For the Little Bunch:
the old gang, the new guard, and so many
who made it in but not out.

LITTLE BUNCH OF MADMEN ELEMENTS OF GLOBAL REPORTING

×

MORT ROSENBLUM

A
Quick
Word

introduction

It is tempting to ignore far-off news. With so much already clouding our line of sight, who needs more problems beyond the horizon? Yet, as British commentator Andrew Marr puts it, free people either play a part in shaping their common destiny or they are deserters.

This little book is for those not prepared to desert. It is aimed at journalists and students who look beyond borders, but also anyone else who wants to keep track of a complex world.

Wherever we turn, someone is redefining news. Reporting, we're told, will be an unpaid hobby as "content" comes fast and free from the ether. Already, readers can pick only what looks appetizing, as at a dim sum lunch. Guesswork and outright lies go unchallenged. Editors offer interactive feedback and have-it-your-way news. Russia invades Poland: what's your opinion?

Anyone in our wired world can add scope and detail to distant stories. Yet anyone can also get things wrong at the speed of light. Journalism is a craft with essential skills, a vocation of bedrock principles and ethics. To report, you have to be there.

H.R. Knickerbocker, a star Hearst correspondent, observed in the 1930s: "Whenever you find hundreds of thousands of sane people trying to get out of a place and a little bunch of madmen struggling to get in, you know the latter are newspapermen."

Today, there are also plenty of madwomen, and newspapers are a dwindling part of it. Our tools are far better now. That struggle may mean simply braving a Roman cab ride. Still, nothing essential has changed.

I have drawn from my own lifetime of reporting but also from generous colleagues of a dozen nationalities who share a basic view: What matters is the message. The challenge is to get it right within a context of history and humanity. The rest is only process.

M.R.
Paris

Cotton
Underwear

chapter one

Back in the proto-technology days, when foreign corre-spondents spent weeks out of touch with their desks, I asked friends what advice editors had offered them as they headed out on their first assignment. Bob Sullivan, as a kid off to an ugly war taking shape in Vietnam for United Press International, went to a promising source. His foreign editor, a gravelly voiced, gray-haired legend named Walter Logan, had been everywhere. "Cotton underwear," Logan told him. "Nylon clings in the tropics."

That was it. The Oracle's wisdom was limited to avoiding sweaty privates. At least Logan came up with something practical. Others' wisdom was basically, "Keep your head down," which is no way to watch news take shape.

Today, guidance is more vital than ever. At the extreme, it saves lives. It can mean the difference between inspired insight and getting things dead wrong. Yet it is hard to find. Fewer editors have been there themselves. Sea-soned hands write great books, but not many explain the basics. Heroic memoirs come from TV or online celebrities.

If old-style jobs are scarce, new niches abound. The world is wide open to young people curious enough to go cover it. And what other pursuit takes you to places you never imagined, shows you life at its limits, and lets you travel among exotic cultures without having to kill anyone? It is, however, a tough pursuit to learn on the job.

This is the manual I wish I'd had back in the 1960s when I was dropped into Congolese mayhem, clueless, sleepless, and scared witless. Much of the Congo spoke French, but I didn't. My sister Jane, only half joking, cracked: "You'll have to say the guy is dead because you don't know the word for wounded." With a measure of luck, I emerged intact. But my work, not to put too fine a point on it, was pathetic. Trial and error is no way to cover events that help shape the course of a planet.

This is also the primer I wish people back home could have had at hand as they puzzled over our dispatches and watched television newscasts. However good correspondents might be, distant readers and viewers tend to miss the point unless they understand the process of newsgathering. In a changed world, we need new frames of reference. Hardly anything now remains within boundaries. "Us" and "them" are over. The Internet removes lines that once separated domestic from foreign news. Hits come from everywhere. Post something about Brazilians or Britons in Fargo, North Dakota, and you may hear from lawyers in Rio de Janeiro or Manchester.

Reporting today must span societies, striking familiar universal chords yet explaining differences. On a recent flight with the pope, a Japanese correspondent stopped Jim Bittermann of CNN. "I'm embarrassed to ask this," he said, "but what are the Ten Commandments?"

Parts of this book are simple tips for the road. When a grim case of Goma-guts strikes at midnight, it helps to have ample flashlight batteries and dysentery pills. Other parts are layered and complex, equally useful to readers back home. All of it applies whether the medium is words on paper, photos, or the fast-morphing panoply of multimedia.

After a few hours in the damp-rag climate of the Congo, I figured out undergarments on my own. During the years that followed, I have thought a lot about the rest of it. In short, the essence is this: Reporters must get up the road. And if possible, they should be there before the story is a story. If they're not there, neither are we.

x

Much has changed, obviously, as we moved from Morse code to modems and on to the mobile phones that allow us to report in real time from the backside of nowhere.

In Africa during the 1960s, we wrote stories on long yellow telegraph forms and handed them to clerks we spent hours befriending, badgering, and bribing. These were cables, named because each waited for space on underwater lines that linked far-flung outposts to London or New York and beyond. At its best, the network was patchwork. A single phone line linked Liberia to the rest of the world via Akron, Ohio — to Firestone, where all the rubber went.

The Associated Press man I replaced in Kinshasa had recently heaped money on a postal clerk to send an urgent cable before closing time on Friday. The guy clipped it to a string hanging from the broken pneumatic tube that once had whooshed cable forms upstairs. He banged on the tube so his colleague a floor above would haul up the string and start punching. When my colleague returned on Monday morning, he found the dispatch still dangling on the clip.

But I lucked out. The post office had just installed the latest modern marvel: Telex machines. These were dull-brown or gray hump-backed monsters, typewriter-creatures whose genes had gone wild. You punched a keyboard, with much clattering and thumping. As words appeared on a paper roll, a thin yellow tape emerged, perforated with dots and flecked with those hanging chads later made famous in Florida voting booths.

If you made a mistake, you reversed the tape and hit the downshift repeatedly to neutralize the offending holes. Then you started over. When ready, you begged an operator for a line to your control bureau in Europe or New York. If the gods smiled, the machine kicked to life within an hour. Heaven forefend you should forget a crucial fact or get something wrong. Lines could suddenly go dead for days.

On my first night in Kinshasa, I pecked at a French keyboard in a tiny room. A censor leaned over my shoulder, breathing secondhand beer and weaving unsteadily as he dandled a Belgian assault rifle. He demanded that I explain the words he did not understand, nearly every one. I ran the tape into a slot, and keys tapped out my story at the blinding speed of 60 words a minute.

Three decades later, when Mobutu Sese Seko fell amid chaotic gunplay, I ducked behind market stalls and dictated a running account over a cell phone to New York. For photos in the 1960s, we needed pigeons. We packaged unprocessed film, went to the airport, and found a reliable-looking stranger headed for Europe who, unless he forgot or got too busy, called the bureau on arrival for a courier to come collect it. (Do not try this today.)

During Nigeria's Biafra War in 1969, it took me four days to get film from the Onitsha front to the nearest AP transmitter. When Pope John Paul II landed at Onitsha in 1998, AP photographer Jerome Delay tossed me his first pictures on a disk. He kept shooting while our satellite-linked computer delivered pictures to papers around the world before the pope descended the aircraft steps. A decade later, even that was Stone-Age technology.

Yet for all this, the basics have not changed since some nameless correspondent ghostwrote Caesar's letters from Gaul. Runners carrying papyrus rolls eventually got to those ancient newsrooms. Today, satellites and fancy electronics make real time the routine, obviating mid-dlemen. But what counts, as always, is the essence.

Now, as then, reporting must begin while a story is still taking shape from fragmented bits as in a revolving kalei-doscope. Otherwise, it is too late to matter.

The technology that speeds our lives is not as simple as it seems. It can go horribly wrong, leaving you lost in the wilderness. For that call I made from Kinshasa, I had spent hours scoring a local cell phone, wheedling and passing out banknotes just like in the good old days.

Progress works both ways. It is easier now for a reporter to move fast and amass information. And, for a lot of reasons, it is also harder. Jacqueline Sharkey, an uncommonly skilled reporter who heads the University of Arizona's journalism school, sums up the challenge:

Your mission is to tell the truth without fear or favor. That's very simple, and it is so difficult. You will find your efforts blocked at every turn — by governments, by people with political agendas, by people who are afraid to talk to you, by people who are afraid of what

you'll say to others, by editors who don't get
what the story is, by news organizations with
special interests in the area you are covering
and are afraid of offending somebody, by fear
of offending advertisers. Your job of telling
the truth is going to be met with innumerable
obstacles.

×

As a correspondents' field guide, nothing surpasses *Scoop*,
that painfully accurate spoof Evelyn Waugh wrote in
1937 after covering Ethiopia. It is the perfect manual
on how not to be a foreign correspondent.

William Boot, the hapless neophyte turned hero, was based
on Bill Deedes, the British journalist who died in 2007 at
94 while still at work. Deedes' last column, written a day
before his death, lamented that the world had failed to
grasp reality in Darfur, not far from where Boot reported
for the Beast.

"You've got a lot to learn about journalism," Boot's old-
hand pal Corker advised him on a slow boat to Ismailia.
"Look at it this way. News is what a chap who doesn't
care much about anything wants to read. And it's only
news until he's read it. After that it's dead."

Tidy little wars sold papers. If the pack couldn't find a
revolution in progress, their hyped-up cables helped to
ignite one. A scoop splashed across the front page meant
fame and modest fortune. Long afterward, when the truth
finally limped in, no one bothered to notice.

News is a product today, as it was then. It competes in
a tough market. In front offices, executives ponder
ways to sell papers, entice viewers, attract listeners,
or rack up hits. Lord Copper, Boot's publisher, didn't
much care if his flash-in-the-pan protégé was the real
deal. Nor do many corporate executives today. They deal
in "content."

Yet to reporters worth the name, content is a swear word. Their own heroes, the people they know and work with, earn their accolades the hard way. Covering real news takes thought, effort, and intricate layers of knowledge. Early correspondents wrote out dispatches in quill pens. Photographers joined their ranks in the 1900s, and TV crews followed a few generations later. Multimedia adds fresh dimensions. Still, practitioners of all sorts can be defined by a simple term: reporters.

Robert Cox, as editor of the *Buenos Aires Herald* in the 1970s, was among the great reporters of our time. In an autobiography so humble that he asked his son to write it, Cox observes, "I have always believed in impersonal journalism, the reporter in a shabby raincoat that nobody notices who writes his stories without a byline." Working just that way, typing late into the night on a battered portable, he exposed the Argentine generals' Dirty War and the silent complicity in Washington.

Typewriters have gone the way of quills and cables, and new technologies have replaced them, but these tools do not change what really counts. The best reporters working abroad may not admit it even to themselves, but they share a calling, a sort of mission imbued with a certain perverse nobility to get it right whatever the circumstance. When a story matters, this band of brothers, and sisters, remembers over decades who reported what.

I can just hear old pals guffaw upon reading that last paragraph. Yes, I use "nobility" advisedly. Reporters also have fun on the road. They sometimes eat well and sleep in fancy places. Pay can be pretty good. Still, I cannot name any reporter I learned to respect over the years who does the job for the money.

The old-style lifers are dwindling fast, like medieval monks clustering around a dying fire. The versatile breed that replaces them is a far more varied crowd, and distant readers must figure who's who among them. This is no easy challenge. It does not help when we confuse improved technology with better coverage.

Twitter, for instance, can tell us a lot in few words. But in Boot's day, correspondents devised their own short-cut language. "Cablese" saved money, and we used it until the 1960s when telex spared us.

Here is a sample in 137 characters, with room for a polite signature:

"PROBOOT EXSALTER ADVISE MILDUDES UPSTICK EMBEDS POOLS REMIND RIGHTSBILL ETRELAY EDPOLICY FREE ACCESS BATTLEFIELD RISKS OUR RESPONSIBILITY REGARDS BEAST"

Translated, that says: From Salter to Boot. Please tell military authorities you reject their plans (i.e., tell them to shove it) for embedding or pools. Educate them on the Bill of Rights and make clear that our editorial policy demands that we have access to the battlefield. We accept any consequences.

If a critical mass of editors had delivered that message early in 2003 as war loomed in Iraq, the world might look considerably different today. Journalists do not make policy, but they are crucial to policymaking. Citizens who elect leaders to keep them safe and prosperous need to understand the world. A competent press corps is no less important than a standing army.

In an old England of nobles, clergy, and commoners, the press was the Fourth Estate. It is the same now in America where three branches of government often fail to check and balance one another. If crucial at home, reporters are even more important abroad where citizens cannot see events that shape their lives.

With an Internet browser, and fingers, anyone can chime in with an opinion, informed or not. But no one can get at truth secondhand. Real reporters need to poke at it, smell its breath, and check its vital signs.

×

Being there is just the beginning. In math, right and wrong
are crystal clear. Reporting is an inexact science. Rémy
Ourdan, a grand correspondent who for a time was foreign
editor of *Le Monde* in Paris, chuckled when I told him I
was writing this. "If I had had your book when I started
in the Balkans, I wouldn't have read it," he said. "I wanted
to learn for myself. I filed stories every day from Sarajevo,
and I could go for months without talking to the desk.
They expected me to tell them what was going on."

This is an emblematic French style. When it works, it is an
excellent way to report. Facts absorbed by osmosis and
telling human detail lead to conclusions. But it takes a
rare gift to pull off. Done wrong, it is editorializing. In
any case, it must be accompanied by stories from others
with official quotes, numbers, and global context.

More often, it is the other extreme. No sooner than a
plane full of reporters lands than the cell phones emerge.
Progress to the hotel is dutifully tracked; interviews
are discussed in advance and analyzed afterward. One of
these days, I expect to hear someone at dinner ask an
editor whether to order the linguini or the lamb chops.

Keith Richburg of the *Washington Post* got the balance
right. When he left Paris to be foreign editor, he reversed
what had gotten to be standard practice. "I would call up
correspondents and ask them what the story was instead
of telling them what we thought." he said. "I told them
to write what they see. That's why they are there."

As news organizations remake themselves, editors with
tight budgets look for eager young people to do it the
Rémy Ourdan way. Penniless in Paris, he scraped up the cash
for train fare to the Dalmatian coast. He appropriated a
car — OK, he stole it — for the drive to Sarajevo. Reckon-
ing with the owner would come later. A French radio paid him
well. Within two years, Le Monde hired him to join a staff
of seasoned reporters who came up in more classic ways.

Shortcuts are the fastest way to get started, but only in the most unusual of cases are they the best. Journalists require no licenses, happily enough. Yet journalism is a profession, or least a craft. A physician's mistake can kill a patient. But reporters can help to trigger, or to prevent, a world war that kills millions.

"Fair and balanced" has been hijacked by an American network with scant regard for either. Yet each has essential meaning. Ourdan waded in as a self-taught swashbuckler, but he quickly grounded himself in the ethics and tenets that define real reporters.

When we graybeards started out, the conceit was that any decent cop reporter could cover foreign news. You just had to be curious, skeptical, energetic, and hungry for the front page. We know better now. Domestic experience helps, but when reporters venture into foreign territory the challenges are immeasurably greater.

A grasp of history, economics, and political science is a basic prerequisite. Smart reporters off to a story, breaking or otherwise, use every possible moment to assemble background. Google is only a start. Without a clear idea of players, issues, and wider context, they are no more than stenographers who cannot help being misled by sources and getting it wrong.

x

Reporting beyond borders demands serious dedication. Lots of people are committed to their work, but this is different. "Off-duty" is not part of the deal. An unexpected phone call can mean racing to the airport as Thanksgiving turkey aromas waft from the oven. Overnight assignments can last for months.

Experience is no guarantee of solid work. Age, gender, nationality, and past profession are beside the point. Dull senses seldom sharpen over time. Practice makes permanent but not necessarily perfect. Some people get it

right from their first day. What counts is commitment to
the story and the ability to tell it dispassionately —
with passion.

The question I am most often asked is: How do you handle
seeing so much violence and death? The answer is to find
the right emotional distance. If you step too far back,
your reporting lacks humanity. If you get too close, emotion overwhelms you.

At times, you help with first aid or a drink of water. But
be very cautious. You are there to witness history and
not to make it. In a Saigon between wars, the AP reporter
Malcolm Browne watched a Buddhist monk calmly douse
himself with gasoline from a plastic bottle and then flick
a lighter. Browne nearly knocked the flame out of his hand.
But he hesitated: he was there for a purpose. He took
photos and wrote stories that showed early on why no
outsiders could remake Vietnam.

After the 2010 Haiti earthquake, some TV reporters appeared to seek out their own personal victims to comfort
and assist — and then to use as props for a dramatic
standup. If in rare circumstances you choose to inter-
vene, tell your camera crew to shoot something else. It
is not about you.

A good reporter from any culture is defined by this ability
to move in close, to listen carefully, and then to step
back to tell the world something new that it needs to
know. How the story is delivered is beside the point. Speed
in most cases is secondary. Yet again: It is all about the
message.

COTTON UNDERWEAR

Learn Languages; Start With Your Own

chapter two

If you're lucky enough to do it, sit down one night with Alison Smale and a magnum of good red wine. Run a recorder. You'll want to remember the conversation, and you won't, I promise, be able to keep up. In posh tones, punctuated by easy laughter, wisdom pours out in torrents. On one such night, Smale talked about why the essence of any good journalism is conveying multiple levels of a story in language that resonates among readers and listeners.

"For centuries, people have been telling each other stories in a certain way," she said. "The reason we invent, that we have these words in languages – the only thing that distinguishes us from animals – is to describe the very fine points of human interrelations. I'm not sitting here being a grumpy old woman; I'm not against the new methods we have to amplify and add to the language. But if we lose the old forms of communication, we will gradually lose what distinguishes us from animals."

Smale had just interviewed Vaclav Havel in Prague. She knew him from his dissident days, and the two of us covered his sudden rise from playwright to president in 1989 when nearly a million moist-eyed Czechs mobbed Wenceslas Square to rattle keys in the air, a goodbye gesture to Moscow. She worked for AP then but later joined *The New York Times* as deputy foreign editor. Now she is executive editor of the *International Herald Tribune.*

Havel had something he wanted to say. And, being Havel, he wanted a reporter he knew would reflect his perfect-pitch nuance. Smale's piece began like this:

PRAGUE – It was supposed to be an interview mulling over the revolution that overturned communism 20 years ago in Europe. But Vaclav Havel, man of words and unshakable determination, had a question.

Was it true, he wanted to know, that President Obama had refused to meet the Dalai Lama in Washington?

Mr. Havel is a fan of the Dalai Lama, who was among the first visitors to Prague's storied castle after Mr. Havel moved in there as president, the final act in the smooth, swift revo-

lution of 1989 that almost seemed scripted by
this playwright-politician for a country that
abhors violence and knows the dark humor of
the absurd. A picture of the Dalai Lama is
displayed prominently on the bookcase greeting
visitors in Mr. Havel's current office in central Prague.

Informed that Mr. Obama had made clear he
would receive the Dalai Lama after the first
presidential visit to China in November, Mr.
Havel reached out to touch a magnificent glass
dish, inscribed with the preamble of the United States Constitution – a gift, he said, from
Mr. Obama, who visited in April.

"It is only a minor compromise," Mr. Havel
said of the nonreception of the Tibetan leader. "But exactly with these minor compromises
start the big and dangerous ones, the real
problems."

"This is actually the first time I really do
mind something Obama did," Mr. Havel said. He
minded it 'much more' than Mr. Obama's recent
decision not to station elements of a missile-
defense system in the Czech Republic, a move
that several Central European politicians
criticized but that Mr. Havel noted was ultimately "an internal American decision."

One day after his 73rd birthday, with a half-
drunk glass of Champagne at his side in mid-
afternoon, the man who steered the Czechs and
Slovaks out of communism showed that his mor-
als, and his sense of mischief, were intact.

Smale went in without a photographer, realizing that a
camera would break the mood. I often joke that for
writers the right word is worth a thousand pictures. Smale

knew her subject as a master at finding the exact language to cast an image, to slam down a sledgehammer
with subtle understatement. Photos of Havel portray an
aging cancer survivor with worry lines. Smale depicted him
more accurately: buoyant.

Havel's English is powerful and poetic. But in Czech his
artfully turned phrases leave the best of translators
befuddled. It is a rich idiom, full of hidden treasures.
Every language has its own little verbs that snap, crackle,
and pop. All have complex constructs and subtleties to
convey ranges of meaning. Whichever ones you write and
speak, journalism demands putting them to good use.

The best reporting takes us nowhere without precise words
that let us see, hear, and feel why it matters. Nothing kills
credibility faster than misspelled words, malapropisms, and
mangled syntax. And nothing builds trust like intelligent
wordplay that sketches textured pictures. For this, you
need an uncommon command of languages. The world speaks
in thousands of tongues, and no one can begin to learn
even all of the main ones. But it is important to hear
inflection and interpret nonverbal clues.

New tools add immediacy and imagery to events that shape
the world. This is a mixed blessing. Smale and I first worked
together in 1982 when Princess Grace died as her car
missed a turn on the steep switchbacks into Monaco. As
the great and famous came to Monte Carlo for a state
funeral, police kept cameras at a distance. Reporters
sketched pictures with words, blending raw emotion with
broader meaning. Looking back, interviews with mourners
showed with enduring power what it meant for the world
to lose its last fairytale princess.

Smale and I talked 20 years, almost to the day, after the
Berlin Wall fell. She was in the East, and her perfect German
picked up telltale undertones in party officials' blather.
She rushed to Checkpoint Charlie. Word raced through
the crowd: the wall had opened. As people paused, stunned
with disbelief, Smale grabbed the young German woman

she had been interviewing. They were the first to cross into the West.

All the wild ebullience — the beeping of tinny Trabant horns, the banging with pickaxes at a hated wall, the hugging and whirling in circles with strangers — was over within hours. Mad scrambles to reach Berlin from Frankfurt or Hamburg were too late.

"Can you imagine what I would have missed if I had been twittering instead of living that moment?" Smale asked. As an answer, she shuddered.

As the level sank in the last bottle of a decent Medoc, I brought up my own pet theme: societies are far more alike than they are different, and each has much to tell the others. Smale nodded.

"Yes," she said, "so long as they talk in the same narrative. If we are really abandoning the way that we tell each other stories then we are truly losing it. No question in my mind. We will have changed something fundamental. Maybe we are reaching hundreds of millions more people than before. But I really think we are on the road to hell."

×

As silly as this may sound in countries that take primary education seriously, reporters must command their own native tongue: grammar, spelling, sentence structure, and all the attendant fine points. Sloppy spelling and frac-tured syntax are dead giveaways to educated readers. Journalists who don't trouble to get their own idiom right carry little authority.

A student once told me writing was not so important to her; she was going into television. Wrong. In broadcast journalism, writing skills are more important than in print. What you leave out says as much as what you put in.

Listen carefully to broadcast newscasts. Stories are

often streamlined to such simplicity that they lose all meaning. Giving general labels to individual players in complex dramas — "the terrorists," for instance — is like giving ball scores without saying who scored what. Airtime is limited; every word counts.

The same principle applies to print, from news briefs to long magazine pieces. For years, I argued that it was better to be a good reporter who writes badly than a good writer who cannot report. A solid desk could whip dispatches into reasonable shape. But no editor could add firsthand observations that were not there to begin with.

These days, it is different. Reporting often goes straight to a broad public untouched by human hands. Sometimes editors arrogate to themselves the reporter's role, writing in passages from what they have seen online or television. And more, news these days is simply too important, too liable to shake economies and skew politics to be misunderstood because of sloppy language.

Good writing, like musical skill, takes an ear. Yet there is a difference. My guitar teacher, nearing suicidal frustration, suggested I take up the iPod. Tone-deaf writers, however, can learn to craft sentences that carry forward narrative, with hard facts set into background color. Pretty is not the goal. Aim to tell your story.

Think before you write, or speak. One American TV reporter in Rome wrote that a new pope had a degree in technology. His editor in New York, vetting the script, corrected that to theology. Powerful as it may be, technology is a false god.

For a class exercise, I put on a helmet and flak vest to brief students as "Colonel Beau Chitlin." Besides several who, without checking, spelled the first name like body odor and guessed at the last, two of them wrote "kernel." Their spell check saw no mistake. If you can't tell a military officer from microwave popcorn, try advertising.

×

Alison Smale could have been equally vivid in Russian, German, or French. Like all good reporters, she learned multiple tongues less because she thought they would be useful than because she wanted to live as an insider among the societies that spoke them. Still, usefulness is a pretty strong reason.

Reporters must communicate with the people they cover. I usually get a laugh when I tell students to learn French and Spanish and then some foreign languages. But that is no joke. Even if English is getting to be the world's lingua franca, non-native speakers express their thoughts more comfortably and completely in their own tongue.

However good interpreters may be, they miss crucial elements. They are an inhibiting presence. People are wary enough of an outsider in their midst. An interpreter, who might be reporting back to authorities or distorting their words, is bound to influence what they decide to say.

Language defines a society. The Spanish see a butterfly as a lyrical fluttering of syllables: *mariposa.* For no-nonsense Germans, it is a *Schmetterling.*

Edward Cody of the *Washington Post* is eloquently polyglot. Back in the 1970s, a star AP reporter chided him for working on his Arabic when he was posted to Beirut. "Our stuff is so shallow you won't need it," the guy said. Cody speaks perfect Arabic, Chinese, and, of course, French and Spanish. His Hindi and Hebrew are spotty. He grew up in rural Oregon, but a teacher got him a scholarship to Florence, and he kept on moving. His first wife was French; his second, Israeli; his third, Chinese.

To capture the essence of global reporting, pick a few correspondents you admire and analyze why. Ed Cody is a dead obvious model. Hardly one to buckle a swash, he speaks so softly you have to strain to hear him. He fades quietly into any background. But his gaze moves constantly, like a raptor looking for lunch. When Cody's eyes get that gleam and his mouth twitches, grab a notebook and follow him.

Lots of people speak foreign languages. But Cody mastered the ability to use linguistic nuance as a means to cross cultural bridges. This is a fundamental skill. It requires shedding personal baggage — perceptions and value judgments — in order to see events through the eyes of others. It takes explaining those events in the context of distant readers. Language skills are the key to this, not only for communicating but also for understanding how societies construe their own worlds.

There are also practical aspects, such as talking your way out of trouble. Some years back, an Israeli radio report attributed to Cody something he didn't write. Nonetheless, Syrian authorities refused for years to give him a visa. Finally, in Lebanon, Cody played his hole card. He visited the information minister, a Palestinian, and announced, "*dakleelak.*" I have entered your territory. Ergo, you as a great man are bound to help me out. The minister, touched by his sense of the culture, prevailed on Syria to give him a visa.

Cody started with AP in the 1970s, in India and the Middle East. When I needed a news editor for the Paris bureau in 1978, I fought hard to get him. Before long, the *Post* offered him a job. He reported from just about everywhere before coming back to run the foreign desk. Then he went out on the road again.

He offers simple advice: write with authority. "You see so many reporters who lack confidence in themselves, who won't step out of the framework set for them by governments," he said. "That kills reporting." And he has a perfect example.

When he moved to El Salvador from the Middle East in 1984, guerrillas dotted the countryside. The story was about how well American advisers were preparing the Salvadoran army to quell them. A colonel briefed reporters regularly, with maps and charts to show increasing success.

"He was a nice man, glib and quick on his feet, and because of his personality the story turned around him," Cody said. "But I was there. It was Christmas, and the entire Salvadoran army went home. There was nobody to man the roadblocks so I drove around the country for three days. I saw where the army was in control and where it couldn't go. Then I went to the house dissident at the American embassy. He laughed and said, 'You figured it out.' Guerrillas controlled two-fifths of the country."

Washington was forced to admit he was right, and El Salvador was suddenly a war to take seriously. Cody had simply dropped in, carefully peeled back the layers, and reported what he saw. His command of Spanish was crucial to the first part. But his evocative use of English brought the story home.

×

Learning to speak a language well depends on a particular arrangement of brain cells. It is easier for some than others, and slow progress should not discourage. Some is better than none.

When I first got to Paris, the AP news editor was a fine journalist and a very smart man. Even after 25 years in France, his accent still sounded like one of those spoofs the French do of tourists stumbling over a phrasebook. Yet his grammar was flawless and his vocabulary vast. He understood everyone and everything. That is what counts.

Your purpose is not to show off for friends. Americans who take pride in their aspirated elisions usually lose it, amusingly, on a booby-trap "r." Gender rules are complex, but who cares if a turnip is male or female? A reporter only needs to communicate and to understand.

This is a lot easier with Romance and Germanic languages

that share much with English. Mandarin Chinese has four tones; Cantonese has nine. The same word, delivered at varying pitches, might get you a cold beer or a belt in the chops. In Nigeria you don't learn Nigerian. Beyond its three main languages, the 150 others include a colorful sort of lilting English.

Just do your best. The more comfortable you are in a language not your own, among people with strange habits and codes to live by, the easier it is to step outside of yourself to see the world for what it really is.

Cultural Bridges

chapter three

If you are lucky, your byline is Ahmed O'Goldberg Wong-Gonzales. Take it from a guy named Rosenblum. However you sign your copy, someone will make assumptions and look for hidden motives or biases. Understand this, deal with it, then ignore it.

Foreign correspondents have belief systems, political leanings, and complex inner workings shaped by family, friends, and societies in which they were raised. To do the job right, we each have to take stock of these various elements and box them away as best we can.

Hard as it was at the time, television anchors in New York should not have cried on camera when the towers fell. That was a time for hard questions from clear-eyed professionals. A stricken nation needed a calm assessment of reality to prevent exactly what occurred: a degradation of the Constitution and blind-fury reactions that ultimately did far more damage than a dramatic but one-time terrorist attack.

At work, reporters are not Americans, or Slovenes, or Buddhists, or Freemasons, or vegetarians. Judges face a similar challenge of suppressing bias. But they can weigh only the evidence put in front of them. If necessary, they can recuse themselves. Reporters on a story must do the work of police investigators and attorneys as well as the judge. And no one else can sit in to replace them on the bench.

Forget that unattainable goal of objectivity. Think instead of fair and balanced. Fox News branders arrogated that phrase to themselves for a reason. That is what journalists are supposed to be. It says that all sides (there are rarely only two) are given consideration. Any judgment, implied or explicit, is based on an honest evaluation of observable facts.

This evenhanded approach is fundamental to any reporting beyond borders. I hammer away at the phrase, cultural bridges, for a particular purpose. Bridges run in two directions. Correspondents might report back to a single newspaper or a global network. If they get it right, their dispatches resonate on both sides of any bridge. Faraway readers form an accurate picture, and people can recognize themselves.

Americans and Europeans tend to regard "foreign reporting" as a one-way lens focused mainly on an ill-defined,
often obstreperous "Third World." That leaves out half
of the picture. Consider, for instance, Vaiju Naravane of
The Hindu, who looks back from her base in Paris.

Her profile of France's new urban poor was headlined, "A
Lingering Aftertaste of Grease and Detergent." One woman
she visited made her coffee but had no hot water to wash
the cups. Poverty is not about geography. When Vaiju
wrote about Gypsies, the Rom, she added a key element
that Western reporters often miss: they are tribal nomads
from Orissa and elsewhere in India, and their wanderings
say much about how migrations define the world.

"I am completely mad," Vaiju told me, with a happy laugh.
She studied with Irish-American nuns in the Himalayas and
then went to Macalester College in Minnesota before
returning to India to study journalism and political science.
She outraged her Brahmin family by marrying a Sikh, whom
she divorced to marry a Frenchman. After another rela-
tionship, with an Italian, she settled down with a French
intellectual who thinks as freely as she does.

She worked for the *Times of India* but switched to *The
Hindu*, still owned by the family that founded it in 1878 to
rankle the British. It circulates 1.4 million copies a day
across India, nearly as many as *The New York Times* and
Washington Post combined, and staffs 17 foreign bureaus.
N. Ram, the director and editor-in-chief, Oxford-educated
with a Columbia journalism degree, is often out on the
street reporting. *The Hindu* hires 30 to 50 graduates each
year from its own journalism college. Its secret to success
is delivering serious news to a society that wants it.

For readers anywhere in the world, papers like *The Hindu*
(www.thehindu.com) are just a few keystrokes away. They
are a rich source for the texture and revealing detail
missing from generic reporting.

"When I write about Pakistan, I have to get into the politics and economics," Vaiju said, "but in the Balkans, for instance, India has no strategic interests. I write about the women, the children, and their lives. Human beings are much more interesting than bombs."

Vaiju is not really mad. Thoughtful and thorough, she teaches journalism at France's prestigious university, Sciences Po. She is a stickler for context and accuracy. "You can't talk about the Poles if you don't know about the First Kingdom or the Second Kingdom and all of that," she said. "If you mention the Geneva Convention, you better have read it. You have to go primary sources and study documents for yourself."

Like correspondents everywhere, she worries that too many unseasoned neophytes are getting news wrong. Without resident reporters, she said, "you don't get the vision of a person you've come to trust, a professionally trained person whose job it is to observe and to tell."

Hard-eyed reporters such as Vaiju offer a reality check for Americans who care about cultural bridges. She admires much about the United States but sees repeated echoes of jingoism she felt during the Iranian hostage crisis in 1979 and 1980.

"Somebody mistook me for an Iranian in a restaurant and started hollering at me, insulting me," she said. "I was utterly shocked. This was part of America's arrogance, ignorance, and emptiness. They tend to project all world ills onto others." It would help, she concluded, if more Americans paid closer attention to other peoples' reality.

×

When I first started reporting from Africa, I asked Bill German, the *San Francisco Chronicle* foreign editor, for guidance on how to capture his attention. "Don't just tell me what happened on a street in Chad," he said. "Tell me what the street looks like." That ought to be chiseled in stone.

William Howard Russell, an ageless model for war correspondents, mastered this skill. He took readers of *The Times*
in London into battles that shaped modern times, from
the Charge of the Light Brigade to the Battle of Bull Run.

Russell reached Turkey in 1854 to spend two years covering
the Crimean War, a calamitous campaign by allied British
and French troops to keep Russia out of the Bosporus.
His dispatches, scrawled in pen and carried to London by
sea, fill a fat book. Here is how he prepared readers for
Gallipoli, a place they would soon know well:

Take the most dilapidated outhouses of farmers' yards in England – remove rickety old
wooden tenements of the Borough – catch up any
seedy, cracked, shutterless structure in our
cathedral towns – carry off sheds and stalls
from Billingsgate, bring them all to the European side of the Dardanelles, and having
pitched on a bare round hill, sloping away to
the water's edge with scarcely a tree or
shrub, tumble them higgledy-piggledy on its
declivity; let the roadway be very narrow, of
varying breadth, according to the bulgings and
projections of the houses, and filled with
large round slippery stones, here and there
borrow a dirty gutter from a back street in
Boulogne – let the houses in parts lean across
to each other so that the tiles meet, or that
a few planks thrown across from over the doorways unite and form a sort of arcade – steal
some Irish round towers – surround them with a
light gallery about twelve feet from the top,
paint them all white, and having thus made
them into minarets, clap them down into the
maze of buildings; transport the ruins into
the centre of the town, with a flanking tower
extending to the water's edge – erect a few
buildings of wood by the waterside to serve as
café, custom- house, and government stores –
and, when you have done this, you have to all

appearance imitated the process by which Gallipoli was created.

After constructing the backdrop, Russell then sketched in the cast of characters:

To fill it up you must, however, catch a number of the biggest breeched, longest bearded, dirtiest, and stateliest old Turks; provide them with pipes and keep them smoking all day on little wooden stages or platforms about two feet from the ground by the water's edge or up the main streets, as well as in the shops of the bazaar (one of the arcades already described); see that they have no slippers on, nothing but shawl turbans, fur-lined flowing coats and bright-hued sashes around the waist, in which are to be stuck silver-sheathed yataghans and ornamented Damascus pistols; don't let them move more than their eyes, or express any emotion at the sight of anything except an English lady; then gather a noisy, picturesque and active crowd of fez-capped Greeks in baggy blue breeches, smart jackets, sashes, and rich vests – of soberly-dressed Armenians – of intellectual-looking Jews, with keen flashing eyes – Chasseurs de Vincennes, Zouaves, British riflemen, vivandieres, Sappers and Miners, Nubian slaves, camel-drivers, commissaries, officers and sailors, and direct them in streams through the streets round the little islets in which the smoking Turks are harboured, and you will do much to populate the place.

Russell followed ill-equipped and badly led British forces to the heights of Balaclava. His readers followed every step, at the edge of their chairs.

At ten minutes past eleven, our Light Cavalry Brigade advanced ... As they rushed toward

the front, the Russians opened on them from
the guns in the redoubt on the right, with
volleys of musketry and rifles. They swept
proudly past, glittering in the morning sun in
all the pride and splendour of war. We could
scarcely believe the evidence of our senses!
Sure that handful of men were not going to
charge an army in position? (...) At thirty-
five minutes past eleven not a British solider,
except the dead and dying, was left in front
of those bloody Muscovite guns.

A century and a half later, memories of that battle remain
fresh. Russell's dispatches brought down the British
Cabinet. He built such elaborate cultural bridges that
Britons understood not only what happened but also why
each part of it happened — and at the hands of whom.

Reporters who get it right often find angry reaction on
one side or the other. In 1860, Russell chose a country
that was famously touchy about how others saw it. He
came to America where many took his mere presence as a
sure sign the North and the South would soon be at war.

As word reached Washington that fighting raged at Bull
Run in July 1861, Russell spent two days finding a horse to
rent. Having settled for two nags and a buggy, he finally
neared the frontlines just as the Union Army came stream-
ing back in retreat. His six- and-a-half-column piece,
published two weeks later, described men "of whom it were
disgrace to the profession of arms to call soldiers"
fleeing wild-eyed from the battle.

Russell acknowledged he was late, but his dispatch was clear
enough. "... the repulse of the Federalists, decided as it
was, might have had no serious effects whatsoever beyond
mere failure ... but for the disgraceful conduct of the
troops. The retreat on their lines at Centreville seems
to have ended in a cowardly route (sic) — a miserable,
causeless panic. Such scandalous behaviour on the part
of soldiers I should not have considered possible, as with

some experience of camps and armies I have never seen even in alarms among camp followers the like of it."

He was also hard on Confederate commanders. Had they pressed their advantage and not stopped short, Russell said, they likely could have overrun Washington.

Union generals conceded he was right. Matthew Brady, the photographer in the thick of it, said his account paled compared to how bad it really was. But when *The Times* reached America, New York newspapers that had covered the debacle a month earlier howled for his skin. Hostility ran to death threats, and Russell took a break in Canada.

American editors dubbed him Bull Run Russell, suggesting he fled in the face of adversity. Stung, he wrote that he knew of no foreigner visiting the United States "who was injudicious enough to write one single word derogatory to their claims to be the first of created beings, who was not assailed with the most viperous malignity and rancor. The man who says he has detected a single spot on the face of their sun should prepare for the winding sheet."

×

Russell's style is purpled with age, but his command of telling detail makes his descriptions timeless. He lamented the advent of telegraph, fearing a push for speed would shove aside substance. And to a large extent, it did. Today's tools can take us to stories as they happen, giving a sense of place along with sights and sounds. Yet they cannot replace a sensitive reporter's own eyes and ears.

Christopher Dickey of *Newsweek* remembers when he covered the Contras and leftist guerrillas in Central American countries which readers up north had such trouble picturing. Joan Didion arrived on her first trip to El Salvador, and they shared a taxi with a young woman. Dickey focused on what the woman had to say; Didion named her perfume. With that simple detail, she was as familiar to distant readers as a similarly scented coworker at the next desk.

Carefully observed and peppered throughout reportage, details paint a picture.

But here is where so many "citizen journalists" go wrong. Anyone can now venture to far-flung places and report back. Russell's readership ran only into the thousands. Today, conceivably, a hobby journalist can reach billions. But the operative word is report. Vivid detail without substantive cultural context is bound to mislead.

Jon Lee Anderson of *The New Yorker* is probably the best all around bridge-crosser in the business. He gets in close to write with intimacy. Then, having the luxury of time and space, he stays there. Anderson lives for weeks, if not months, at the heart of each story. Years afterward, characters in his pieces stay in touch as old friends.

"The first and main principle is to throw yourself in over your head in another culture," he says. "I think that it is so important for a journalist to try to have a sense of other people's humanity, not your own."

Accounts of torture from Abu Ghraib prison in Iraq, for instance, were shocking enough to American readers who knew little of Muslim and Arab societies. But readers who were helped to comprehend the humiliation of sexual taunts by female soldiers or the horror of unleashed dogs knew why anti-American hatred was so deep and indelible.

Anderson, the son of a USAID agricultural adviser, was raised in South Korea, Colombia, Taiwan, Indonesia, and Liberia. At 14, he decided to wander off and get himself lost in the wilds of Africa.

Soon after 9/11, he hurried to Northern Alliance territory in Afghanistan where Osama Bin Laden's agents posing as a TV crew had blown up Ahmed Shah Massoud. This short passage in *The New Yorker*, no more than sidelight color about a minor warlord, gives a clear idea of a strange culture about to enter center stage:

Mamur Hassan is a small sturdy-looking man,
and light on his feet. He has a beard of medium length that is mostly gray, and short-
cropped black hair running to gray as well. He
usually wears a long-tailed tunic and matching
pantaloon outfit – which is what most Pakistani
and Afghan men wear – and, over it, a mili-
tary-style multipocketed vest. He has a wide
nose, and large brown eyes with crow's feet at
the corners. He listens attentively and speaks
with a warm, reedy voice, full of inflection,
in Uzbek or Dari, the Afghan variant of Farsi.
Mamur Hassan appears to be in his late fifties.
Like a lot of Afghans, he does not seem to
have much thought about his age, and when we
first met he told me that his father, who he
said was a hundred and seven when he died two
years ago, was thirty when he was born. I
pointed out that if that was the case Mamur
Hassan would be close to seventy. He hesitated
and began counting on his fingers. He said that
he was born in the Muslim year 1322 – 1943 in
the Christian calendar – and since it was now
1380, he agreed that it was possible that he
was fifty-seven or fifty-eight.

Anderson's palette runs to vivid colors and shades of gray,
with little black or white. He paints in Hassan's two wives,
five children, prayer beads, and his tin case of *naswar*
("the tobacco-spice-herb mixture – a mild stimulant –
that many Afghan men are addicted to.") He adds jumpy
bodyguards and then describes the army Hassan commands.
With that come essential bits of history and geography.

And then, after depicting his interlocutor and displaying
a level of mutual trust, he gets into substance:

I asked Hassan what Islamic state he admired,
or could see as a model for Afghanistan, and
he said that Islam, as he understood it, was a
civilized religion and allowed for states in

which, for example, Muslims and Christians could live together without problems: 'This is the kind of Islamic state we want.' I asked what he felt toward unbelievers. 'I don't think anything,' he said. "I don't mind what they are.'

At first, this seems like no more than a good writer painting pictures with his keyboard. Soon enough, we see Hassan more deeply, layer by layer. Deep in the piece, Hassan tells how Soviet troops killed his mother, two of his four brothers, and five nephews. Hassan had sneaked down from the mountains one night, and his mother slaughtered a goat to feed him and his men. A relative who lived nearby told the Russians, who massacred his family. Hassan explained: "The mujahideen had killed his father, and this was his way of taking vengeance. Later, we caught him and I said to him, 'We killed your father and you killed my mother and that's the end of it.'"

When Anderson expressed surprise at the merciful gesture, Hassan laughed. "Now I am amazed at what I did. But, because of it, this place is secure, and no one threatens me or wants to kill me."

Years later, such reporting remains a useful basis for distant readers. It shows at a glance that simplified generality only confuses and confounds. Anyone who absorbs such insight into this society, with its ancient blood codes and capacity for loss, understands why Afghans are undefeatable by outsiders who do not fathom their depths.

×

My own copy is hardly the standard, but it can serve as an example here because I know the elements behind it.

When Anderson headed north, I got into Kabul to join AP's team already on the ground. A newcomer, I could hardly approach the substance provided by Kathy Gannon, who had followed Afghanistan from the inside out for more than a decade. Her colleague Amir Shah, who started out as a driver with no English, reported on his own culture with uncanny acuity and courage.

My job as special correspondent was to sketch a contextual backdrop for Americans about to venture onto unfamiliar ground. After a quick look around and side-street conversations, I took this approach:

KABUL, Afghanistan — With satellite dishes snipped from tin cans, Afghans can sit back in the Middle Ages and keep tabs on the 21st century. Their bad luck is that this optical miracle works only one way.

"I'm afraid the world just doesn't understand us," Shahla Paryan lamented, pouring the inevitable tea for a visitor sitting on a rich red carpet inside old mud walls. "It is wrong to believe that we were the same as those horrible people who brought terrorism to America," she said. "It is very wrong."

When projected to outsiders, this capital evokes mixed images of One Thousand and One Nights placed in an Old Tombstone movie set. But cameras can't show the dazzling complexities of societies as old as time.

Shahla and her sister Nilofar, for instance, view five years of Taliban rule as a nightmare forced upon them against which they had no defense but to wait behind closed curtains for deliverance.

Both are university graduates who specialize in combating illiteracy, and they are as much a part of the picture as the more familiar women in body-bag burqas who symbolize most Westerners' idea of Afghanistan.

For them, Osama bin Laden was a plague no more
welcome than locusts or cholera. They see the
Arab fighters around him as bullying strangers
with no respect for the Afghans' ancient sense
of right and wrong.

A good look at Kabul reveals the danger of
generalizing about a fiercely independent yet
loosely knit nation of 21 million: Pashtuns,
Tajiks, Uzbeks, Hazara, Turkmen, Sikhs, Hindus.

Streaks of cruelty and fanaticism are marbled
into far more common national ingredients:
hospitality, respect for elders and traditions, self-reliance and the ability to resist
incredible hardship on two cups of tea a day.

"We don't want to see each other as ethnic
groups but rather as individual Afghans who
must solve problems in common," said Mubarak
Ahmed Yar, soft-spoken and gray at 57.

As Afghanistan's director of forestry, Yar
knows political infighting wastes the scant
time the country has left to avert ecological
as well as economic disaster. After 25 years
of war, infrastructure lies in shambles.

But as headman of a neighborhood of worried
Pashtuns at the edge of Kabul, he also knows
that the "broad-based government" now under
discussion is all that can save yet another
generation from war.

If Pashtuns are a minority in Kabul, they are
the most numerous group in Afghanistan. Most
Taliban are Pashtun, creating a sort of guilt
by association that Yar deplores. Like many of
his tribe, he hates the Taliban.

"Those mullahs reduced us to nothing," he

said. "Their rule destroyed what little we had
left — technology, industries, schools, agri-
culture, roads. They were like horses with
blinders pulling us in one direction."

Communal tension has flared periodically in
Kabul's history, now deep into its third mil-
lennium, but its multicultural inhabitants
have built a rich and textured society that is
more often ethnically seamless.

This city of something over a million lies on
a plain ringed by dramatic mountains, snowy in
winter and achingly beautiful in all seasons.

Its old mud heart was pounded to pieces during
shelling and firefights among the warlords who
together drove out Russian troops in 1989,
then turned on each other. Yet much remains to
evoke the ancient flavor of a capital unlike
any other.

Along the noxious trickle of the Kabul River,
market life seems little changed from the
ancient days. Stalls offer luscious pomegran-
ates, gigantic turnips, dates and grains of
every sort. Meat hangs on hooks outdoors.
Open-air barbers still shape long beards and
now also shave chins clean.

Two brown-earth forts loom over Kabul, the
older dating centuries back to Moghul days.
Both are in partial ruin, but each was aptly
suited for its modern purpose: a base from
which to shell the hapless city below.

High on a hill sits a giant white hotel, built
in a more hopeful time for the Inter-Continen-
tal chain. Now, locally owned, it languished
until foreign journalists took it over in
recent weeks.

The Taliban banned music, movies, television, beardlessness and just about anything else they regarded as un-Islamic.

Yet enterprising Afghans made the best of things. A small supermarket offered Oreo cookies and tortilla shells along with such staples as rice and tea. Hole-in-the-wall shops sold mid-tech Asian electronics.

But, suddenly there is dramatic change.

In post-Taliban euphoria, shopkeepers have hauled secret stocks out of hiding. Racy Indian actress pinups decorate shops that blare once-banned music into traffic-choked streets. A few Western fashions are on display.

A gaily painted beauty parlor has opened on a main street, with glamorous photos of hair styles.

Electronics shops are booming, literally and figuratively. Music blares from mega-bass speakers. Merchants sell TV sets by the hundreds, as fast as smugglers can get them over the mountains from Pakistan.

Buyers can spend $200 for a fancy satellite dish or half that much for an ingenious homemade version of flattened cans soldered together.

Leonardo DiCaprio portraits adorn every shop. "Titanic" videocassettes are a best seller, perhaps because Afghans can identify with a spectacularly sinking ship. In the bustle of the electronics market, 12-year Ahmed Siar tried out a new word in his meager English vocabulary: "Excellent."

By the river, laughing kids kick around soccer

balls with amazing energy considering their
jobless fathers can barely afford a single
daily meal. Five dollars a month is a good wage.

One riverbank neighborhood resembles an ar-
chaeological site, bombed to near oblivion
with only bits of jagged wall and the odd
half-roof left to shelter displaced families
who cannot afford to live anywhere better.

Foreign embassies and aid missions are preparing to reopen. The new resources their governments bring should allow families to repair
their collapsing walls. Stability should lure
back overseas Afghans with their savings.

As always, the most reliable economic indica-
tor is the gold market. When times are bad,
people convert plummeting Afghani notes into
hard currency. At the promise of better times
ahead, they are buying gold jewelry.

Jeweler Hamid Aga Jan, 20, is giving some of
his own merchandise to the bride he'll marry
after Ramadan, the Muslim holy month. Two-
thirds of his relatives are in Pakistan, Russia or Germany, 600 in all, but they are returning for the wedding.

As in the old days, the family will rent the
Najib Aziz Hotel, along with a jazz band, for
a proper Afghan wedding. "My family is coming
home," Jan said. "They've just been waiting for
an optimistic time, and we think this is it."

So far, for 2,000 years or so, that has been
Kabul's pattern: ruin and return. With adobe
walls and painted woodwork, new construction
looks centuries old a week after it is done.

Harder to repair is the human damage. Since the

Soviets invaded in 1979, 1.5 million Afghans have died. Some refugees have come home, but 3.5 million remain scattered across the globe.

Millions of land mines still claim lives and limbs. Health statistics put Afghanistan among the world's bottom three nations in child mortality.

More than half of all Afghans have no access to even rudimentary medicine. Few hospitals in cities have medicines. In some, overworked staffs have not been paid for months.

"It is a terrible situation," said Kate Rowlands, who runs Emergency Hospital. "Most of us are worried about AIDS, and they're still struggling with diarrhea."

Still, the overall mood is upbeat.

Shahla Paryan, with her shutters open, wearing an embroidered blue dress and no scarf over her black hair, is grateful to Americans for the change. Her only fear, she said, is that Americans will forget about Afghanistan, as they did after the Soviets were driven out.

"This is our great opportunity," she concluded. "We cannot miss it."

×

That was my first look at Afghanistan, but even in my first year as a correspondent, I had a sense of it thanks to a foreign editor named Ben Bassett. In 1968, he sent all AP bureaus a *New York Times* piece by Joe Lelyveld on buzkashi, take-no-prisoners Afghan polo with a goat carcass as the ball and no discernible rules. Lelyveld portrayed a people: strict order amid chaos, nobility laced with ignoble acts, a toughness of spirit that no outsider was likely to quell.

Every aspect of that trip illustrated challenges I had
seen over earlier decades. Be Prepared might work for Boy
Scouts. But in a wide-open world, be prepared for what?

I had gone to Peshawar from Islamabad for two days,
carrying a change of clothes, my trusty medical kit (more
on this later), assorted notes and numbers, and a laptop.
I ran into Rod Nordland and Gary Knight, *Newsweek*'s
wrecking crew. "Hop in," Gary said. "We're going to Kabul."

At the Khyber Pass, a wild-eyed Pashtun with a vintage
carbine peered into the jeep and saw my Semitic-but-not-
Arabic nose. "*Yahoud*," he yelled. A dozen others rushed
over for a word with the Jewish guy. Rod floored it and
barreled into Afghanistan.

We stopped for a break on the narrow mountain road
above the ancient capital, dawdling over sandwiches we
had scored as Rod raced out of Peshawar so fast he left
his translator-fixer behind. A reporter to his toenails, he
knew getting to the story fast trumped all else. Nothing
seemed amiss; no one's antennae crackled. Hours later, a
roving band seized four journalists at that same spot and
put them all to a horrible death.

Day after day, the received ideas I had brought to Kabul
dropped away. Afghanistan in late 2001 and early 2002
was a textbook study on why generality and presumption
shed so little light on human realities.

Back home, Americans assumed the Taliban's fall would free
Afghan women from crushing male domination. Goodbye to
those humiliating sacks, with tight mesh across the eyes
that filtered out so much of the world. But the garment
predates the Taliban by centuries — millennia, if you add
Persian roots. I went to a burqa shop to investigate.

The place was hopping. A salesman, with that leer peculiar
to beauty pageant hosts, reported no drop in business.
Shoppers chatted like Manhattan housewives at Bloomingdale's. One, who displayed a flash of sexy black lace

stocking between hem and slipper, explained the facts of life. She felt perfectly comfortable wrapped up out of public view, and her husband was happier for it. If she decided to shed it, it would be her choice. Meantime, she was torn between robin's egg blue and a darker regal hue.

Two hours later, I interviewed four fiery housewives who were organizing a march to the center of town. Women would yank off their burqas in unison with symbolic flourish. They had been forced to take cover during Taliban years, and they didn't like it.

As that trip made clear, both correspondents and the people to whom they correspond need a clear sense of geometry. The world is flat only if you observe it from an airplane window at 30,000 feet.

Despite global market forces that suggest otherwise, individuals group into clans and tribes that long ago settled into clearly definable cultures. Each has devised ways of life which air travel and Internet access are not likely to obliterate anytime soon.

In the Old World that Americans know best, European nations have forged a union with common policies and a single Parliament. But look carefully at life on either side of any open border you choose, and judge for yourself. That is only Europe. Beyond, it gets complicated fast.

When you reach deep valleys of the Hindu Kush and peaks defining inaccessible Pakistani tribal territories, you find that "flat" is not a useful concept.

Every detail matters. Being left-handed, I am constantly on guard when Afghan or Arab hosts produce a mealtime platter of meat and rice into which everyone plunges their fingers. Use your left hand — which others in the assembled company reserve for out-house hygiene — and at best you are ostracized as an uncouth kafir. For Thais, in a royal palace or a rice farmer's hut, a poorly aimed shoe sole offends more than a four-letter curse word.

Yet here is that conundrum: however much one culture may differ from another, all people are far more alike than they are different. Mothers want a safe place to put their kids to bed and something to give them for breakfast. Fathers want their families to survive intact, to grow up secure in whatever belief systems they hold.

In my wanderings around Kabul, I happened upon a quiet neighborhood near the airport. Small, well-kept houses lined the dirt streets, the homes of comfortable working families. On one of those streets, a red-eyed man in his forties stared into a gaping crater. It was where his young daughter had been playing hopscotch. U.S. jets attacked the runway, and a not very smart bomb missed by nearly a mile.

The larger issues are complex. Perhaps this was a tragic but unavoidable casualty, what happens when a powerful nation is pushed into justifiable war. But talking to that man, no different from any stricken father anywhere, one thing was dead plain. The cultural bridge between Kabul and Kansas City is barely a few steps long.

Gatekeepers,
Gatecrashers

chapter four

To foreign correspondents, no one looms larger in life than the editor who directs them. A good one can lighten any hardship and turn hurried mishmash into polished prose. A bad one can make Adolf Hitler seem like SpongeBob SquarePants. In any large news organization, there are some of both, with variations in between.

During those introspective 1970s, when many of us began to look hard at world news coverage, we used a descriptive term for editors: gatekeepers.

In all news operations, potential stories crowd the entrance like eager clubbers at a new hotspot. The obvious riffraff are shooed away. Others must be screened; space is limited, whether in print, online, or on air. Even the most attractive prospects get turned away if something essential is missing.

With foreign news, this process is complex. Editors need a clear worldview, preferably based on experience of their own abroad, to know what is important. They must deal with copy from local journalists whose language is not their editors', whose training is spotty, and who may find themselves dead if their stories upset the wrong people.

As scrutiny increased over their vital role, many good editors got better. In a large newsroom, as many as eight sets of hands handled a story before it got through the gate. Smart reporters cultivated helpful editors and learned to avoid the worst depredations of the ham-handed.

But as economic hard times followed ventures into Web-based delivery systems and "citizen journalism," a century-old structure of layered editing was suddenly turned on its head. Now the news business morphs almost overnight. Many editors still perform their essential roles. But we have a new class to consider: gatecrashers.

Business people saw simplified structures as ways to save money. Many regarded editors as expendable middlemen and fired as many as they could. This suited journalists seeking shortcuts to glory who shunned any imposing editorial hand as they might a kibitzing aunt.

In those early days, I wrote several dispatches from India for The Huffington Post, which was on its way to worldwide prominence. It was simple: you posted copy on a template. Hours or days later, your story showed up on the site, seemingly untouched by human hands. To an old reporter, the whole concept was horrifying.

The good part was open access. The press critic A.J. Liebling famously wrote that freedom of the press was guaranteed only to those who owned one. No longer. At the touch of a keystroke, impressive people can say much for free. But in such an operation, who keeps the gates?

A solid story can take weeks, or months, to research and hours more to write. Getting it firsthand can cost thousands in expenses. And, if we write for free, we are no longer professionals whose livelihood depends on getting it right.

So what is our motive? A need to establish ourselves as expert in some field? A desire to contribute knowledge? A bias to promote? Simple ego? In each of these cases, our copy screams for basic fact-checking, let alone a watch on fairness and balance.

Whether seasoned journalists or evenhanded essayists with time on our hands and money in the bank, we will make mistakes.

As editor of the *International Herald Tribune*, I handled copy from reporters I had idolized for decades. Some made gargantuan errors, risking ridicule if not legal action. Many made small ones in need of fixing. Questions had to be asked; developing stories needed updates. This is the norm. Everyone – everyone – needs an editor.

Email exchanges alone are dangerous. Messages are misread, and they can go astray. "Blog teams" are like assembly lines, fine for bolting wheels on a Ford or milking cows in an automated dairy, not for real news that affects human lives.

So I emailed the faceless Huffpost desk until someone replied. I asked him what should happen if I caught a serious blunder after filing. Or suppose there was a crucial update? He finally gave me a phone number but urged me not to use it. That would defeat the purpose, cutting into speed and high volume.

For reporters who sometimes spend weeks in remote places cursing their newsdesks back home in terms unsuitable for textbooks, it seems strange to champion the role of editors. Yet the more gatecrashers undermine public faith in real journalism, the more crucial gatekeepers become.

To see why, it is important to understand how systems used to work before it became so easy to bypass the gate altogether and just climb over the wall.

Coincidentally, though not entirely, change happened fast around a point in time that is easy enough to remember: September 11, 2001.

×

Until 2001, American newspapers, magazines, and networks maintained large staffs worldwide. *The New York Times* and *Los Angeles Times* each based about 35 reporters abroad, with the *Washington Post* not far behind. The *Chicago Tribune,* the *Boston Globe,* the *Baltimore Sun, Newsday,* and the *Miami Herald* had significant foreign services. So did, among others, *Newsweek,* Time, and the three networks. Chains like Knight-Ridder pooled the work of excellent small staffs.

Editors sometimes promoted correspondents from their own newsrooms, but often they raided The Associated Press for their foreign reporting staffs. That was a reasonable guarantee of skilled seasoning. Like Reuters in Britain, AP was set up in the mid-1800s as a globe-spanning cooperative to supply newspapers with coverage they could not afford on their own.

AP hired only reporters who had proved themselves on daily newspapers. After years in a domestic bureau, an aspiring correspondent might make it to the Foreign Desk in New York to wait until someone retired, died, or decided to come home. Almost no one got fired.

New hires needed at least five years of experience on a daily newspaper. Those who stayed the course got the whole enchilada: a living wage with job security, benefits, school for the kids, and home leave.

Since policy was to promote only from within, the CEO (then called the general manager) and all executives had experience in turning out AP's only product: news. Everyone started in a domestic bureau and then worked upward, one promotion at a time. Louis D. Boccardi took over in 1985 as the first chief executive who had not come up through the ranks. He joined AP as a senior editor in 1967 with years of experience on New York dailies.

As a non-profit, AP did its job and at the end of the year its owners — newspapers and broadcasters across the United States — divvied up the bill. To help defray increases in member dues AP also sold its product to subscribers, thousands of news outlets across the world.

By 2001, newspaper publishers saw their profit margins dwindle as print circulation declined and a recession drove away advertisers. Very few were losing money, but shareholders accustomed to annual earnings above 30 percent pushed for the same rich margins. Younger readers preferred their news online, and few publishers found ways to monetize the Web. Most provided "content" for free in hopes of converting hits into paid subscriptions or eyeballs for online ads.

After those aircraft struck on 9/11, the old-style news industry began to crumple as dramatically as the twin towers. It took years rather than minutes, but the eventual result was devastating.

In 2003, the AP board replaced Boccardi with Tom Curley, the 12th chief executive since 1848. He had been president and publisher of *USA Today* since 1991. After four years as night city/suburban editor of the *Rochester (N.Y.) Times-Union,* he moved to Gannett headquarters to coordinate news research projects.

Boccardi had a master's degree in journalism from Columbia University. Curley's master's, from the Rochester Institute of Technology, was in business administration. His mandate was to find new income so the cooperative's members could pony up less to meet its costs.

Working with Kathleen Carroll, hired in mid-2002 from the Knight-Ridder chain to be executive editor, Curley radically changed the way AP covers the world.

Over a few months early in 2004, AP fired or forced into retirement dozens of correspondents and bureau chiefs, with something near 500 years of combined experience. They were too expensive. Some were replaced by fresh hires with low wages and limited benefits.

Most of the dismissed old hands left quietly, bitter and humiliated, and signed confidentiality agreements in exchange for severance. AP's foreign correspondents were paid in New York, where arbitrary dismissal is routine. They had never sought protection from the Wire Service Guild contract that covered domestic reporters. For most, it was a point of pride; they saw their demanding jobs as about more than money.

Laurinda Keys, an American based in India, fought back. Called to London, she thought she was being promoted to replace the departing bureau chief. Instead, she was dismissed after 28 years in 30 countries. Her lawsuit said she was offered a meager pension if she took early retirement at 53; if she refused, AP would not bring her home from India, contrary to standard practice. The agency argued that the court had no jurisdiction and that the suit had an "ulterior motive to harass the management of AP." An Indian judge awarded her $125,000.

In this climate, people kept their heads down and adhered

scrupulously to increased control from New York. Regional editing desks kept them on tight leashes. AP was less of a family where correspondents went extra miles, often at great risk, for a "herogram" from headquarters. This was business.

My own job changed. I had rejoined AP in 1981 after two years at the *International Herald Tribune.* As special cor-respondent, I was assigned to add context and analysis to major stories. In 2003, I filed stories from Jordan quoting Middle East sources on the likely result if America invaded Iraq without broad support, and I tried to draw parallels to Vietnam. Editors in New York, with their own sources, rewrote some stories and spiked others. AP and I separated in 2004.

My own view is that news is best covered by reporters who see it take shape, who know their sources, and under-stand the setting. Editorial control, if essential, should not be overdone. Beyond this philosophical question, however, AP faces a fundamental challenge. Covering an unruly world is expensive and yet too many people now demand news for free.

As Curley sought fresh profit centers to earn revenue, he froze hiring and slashed travel budgets. In 2009, he decimated the overall staff, letting go every tenth person. In 2010, AP reported that its net income had plunged by nearly 10 percent. It expected a decline in 2011 as well, which would be the first back-to-back drop since the Great Depression.

What suffered most was AP's historic mission. With war in Afghanistan, world financial crises, and trouble simmering across the planet, it cut news-coverage expenses by 24 percent. AP would have posted a loss in 2010 had it not sold off its German service, which since the Cold War has been a cornerstone of its European coverage.

More than anytime before, reporters are needed to roam the globe freely and find news no one yet knows is out there. The economic factors facing AP have a similar impact on newspapers and networks.

By 2010, *The New York Times* still had a foreign staff worth the name. The *Los Angeles Times* was down to 14. Some big papers kept a few correspondents on tight budgets. Others closed their overseas bureaus altogether. The *Washington Post* not only gutted its foreign service but also closed bureaus in the United States. Television networks, to a large extent, effectively outsourced the news, picking it up from other outlets as they dramatically cut their own foreign staffs.

In March 2010, the Audit Bureau of Circulations report cast a pall. *The New York Times* weekday sales dropped 8.5 percent to 951,063. The *Washington Post* fell by 13.1 percent and the Los Angeles Times by 14.7 percent. Of all top U.S. dailies, only The Wall Street Journal advanced — by 0.5 percent.

As newspapers and networks cut back, they rely ever more heavily on what 19th-century publishers created: a nonprofit cooperative to cover the world for them. But AP now focuses on big stories and projects that strengthen its brand. Much of its work is excellent: solid scoops by such stars as Charles Hanley and Kathy Gannon. Some young reporters do better work than familiar old hands. AP is strong in America, its staff fired up by Michael Oreskes, a top editor hired from *The New York Times.*

AP can still hit hard abroad, deploying forces no one can match. When red-shirted insurgents paralyzed central Bangkok in 2010, bureau chief Denis Gray tempered eyewitness accounts with wisdom acquired over four decades in Thailand. Anyone could see that their broomsticks and firecrackers were no match for an advancing army. But this was about a deposed populist premier, and Gray knew what might well come next. Bangkok is an AP regional center, flush with talent. Along with hard news and analyses, AP provided video feeds and background packages.

Yet much is left uncovered elsewhere in the world. Small stories fester out of sight until they are too big to ignore — or to mitigate. The demands of new media tie AP reporters to their desks to update websites. Vital time is spent on celebrities and oddities to brighten the report.

Rather than training correspondents at headquarters, AP recruits freelancers already in place or raw interns who can work up the ladder. The trusty old agency was once nicknamed A&P because it was a supermarket of news. Along with fine foods, people need canned beans and sacks of flour. And, like groceries, real news comes at a price.

×

For aspiring correspondents who show promise, these changed circumstances create an opportunity. Doors that could take decades to squeeze through can be pushed open overnight. The tradeoff is that much less awaits them inside.

If mainstream jobs are tough to find, it is easier now to simply go where things are popping and hustle up some business. Many news outlets that have no foreign staff are eager to pretend that they do. Many editors rely on ragtag bands of freelancers — stringers — whom they pay by the piece. Enough bits of string can add up to a reasonable living. Any decent scoop is money in the bank.

This, in fact, is a time-honored practice of mixed worthiness. Into the 1980s, an enterprising stringer in Amman, Jordan, wrote not only for AP but also its competitors and a handful of other outlets. He typed stories in thick carbon sheaves. Whoever had paid him most recently got the top copy.

In Damascus, an oily Syrian who pimped for foreign prostitutes on the side worked for several news outlets. He was also close to Syria's intelligence apparatus. Reporters likely to uncover hard truths saw their visas inexplicably delayed.

This is yet another reason for gatekeepers. Any news organization, big or little, professional or amateur, needs editors to direct reporters, check facts, fill holes, and smooth out copy. They also need editors to protect readers, listeners, and viewers from deliberate lies.

The term, gatekeeper, was chosen well. Each bit of copy must run a gauntlet to be poked and prodded and sniffed before it is allowed off the final editor's desk.

The unsung heroes are copy editors, who once tended to be grumpy old guys with hemorrhoid cushions and fat lead pencils. When I worked at the *Arizona Daily Star* in 1960s, one got so sick of a reporter's excess semicolons that he grabbed a pair of pliers and cut the key off the guy's typewriter.

In this new environment, freshly minted reporters must learn to patrol their own work. Spell check is only a start; remember that military "kernel." Each fact must be tested against a trusted source (not whatever pops up on Google). The slightest doubt about a quote needs checking.

This can go only so far. Writers of any sort, however gifted, should not edit their own copy any more than surgeons should remove their own tonsils. Though technically possible, it is a very bad idea. Yet gatecrashers do it all the time.

My stomach churns when I see experienced people misspell simple words, a clear sign that they pushed the button without going back for a careful read. Getting the basics right is essential to credibility. And credibility is the cornerstone of everything else.

×

The shooting of Neda Agha-Soltan during upheaval in Iran is a clear example of how gatecrashers can contribute enormously but also why gatekeepers are so essential.

As disputed election returns came in during June 2009,

experienced journalists provided solid reporting, with quotes from opposing candidates, street reaction, and thoughtful interviews with Iran's intelligentsia. Then police rounded up reporters, and visas were cancelled.

The story shifted to impressions and images from Iranians with cell phones, concealed cameras, and Twitter accounts. Some comments were brave and incisive. Others were wildly exaggerated. Some was clumsy propaganda. Since citizen journalists must be anonymous in such cases, it was impossible to determine which was which.

Real reporters who evaded the roundup laid low in the early stages. Nearly everyone had to remain unnamed for obvious reasons. News desks had plenty of atmosphere but with little sense of what it really meant.

World attention zeroed in on that chilling sequence: Neda, with her gentle smile and captivating eyes, crumpled into the arms of a friend. Bystanders' lenses defied the authorities who tried to black out Iran.

Neda was a compelling symbol. Her name means "voice" or "divine message" in Farsi. Yet the reaction that followed was based on pure emotion. Such dramatic moments are only puzzle pieces until they are fit in place against a backdrop. Who shot Neda? Was she a protester targeted by an oppressive regime, or was she just in the wrong place? The questions were countless, and most answers were guesswork.

After the texting and twittering subsided, I talked to Stephen Erlanger of *The New York Times,* who first saw Iranians stage-manage events 30 years earlier. He covered the hostage crisis, watching sharply angled TV cameras make a handful of students blockading the U.S. Embassy seem like a 444-day street party. Over the decades, he has watched Iran from the inside, from Arab capitals, and from Israel.

Most anyone seeing that turmoil in Tehran would logically

assume a rejection of the mullahs' theocracy. But Erlanger had seen the power of religion to reshape a society fragmented under the shah.

"People aren't against the Islamic regime, they're against fraud," he said. "This was not a revolution against the government, which doesn't seem to be in danger." But, he added, the tough repression carried a heavy cost. "This was a very serious blow to their reputation abroad. You can see it in Lebanon, in Gaza. No longer can they say democracy and the Islamic revolution are the same."

In vitally important places like Iran, the story is not so much about dramatic outbursts but rather the long haul. Titanic-type mishaps aside, ships of state turn slowly. Wise editors look for local reporters and correspondents with long experience who freshen their contacts with periodic visits. This can be exceedingly difficult.

Iran is particularly good at shading the story, by artful disinformation or brutal example. Three months before elections, the Islamic government arrested Roxana Saberi, an Iranian-American journalist working for NPR and the BBC. She was sentenced to eight years in prison.

On June 21, as crowds protested the election, revolutionary guards rousted Maziar Bahari from bed and tossed him into Evin prison in Tehran. He was accused of spying for the CIA, MI6, Mossad — and *Newsweek.* In Bahari's case, gatekeeper was more than figurative. For 118 days, 12 hours, and 54 minutes he was interrogated, harassed, and tortured. *Newsweek* editors pressed a global campaign that got Bahari released. His head tormenter warned him to say nothing. "We can put people in a bag no matter where in the world they are," the man said. "No one can escape from us." But Bahari defiantly reported the grim details, and he wrote at length of the paranoia that permeates Iran.

The New York Times, which has covered Iran well since the Shah fled in 1979, sent Robert Worth to cover the election. His visa was cut short days after the voting. Roger Cohen held out 10 days longer until June 24, writing poignant columns that drew from an intimate knowledge of Iran. Nazila Fathi, the paper's longtime super stringer in Tehran, continued her coverage.

On June 27, Fathi described eerie stillness in the normally frenetic capital: "Even in areas of the city not known for liberal politics, the sense of frustration, and despair was palpable," she wrote. "Those who accuse the government of stealing the election said they had lost the hope for change they had during the protests that drew tens of thousands of people into Tehran's streets. But others also confessed to feeling depressed."

Then she fled to Toronto after threats to her family. The Times was down to a few local stringers who could not be named. Deprived of access, editors looked in the windows. Peripheral bureaus monitored official broadcasts, and correspondents carefully filtered the polyglot roar from cyberspace. This was when trusted old contacts paid off.

Well-connected Iranians in exile and diplomats with divided sympathies added fresh pieces to the mosaic. Worth wrote from Beirut and Dubai, and Fathi worked her sources from Canada. In the background, seasoned correspondents put a frame around a story they had watched since Ayatollah Khomeini swept in from France in 1979. Elaine Sciolino, who wrote a classic book on Iran, filed from Washington. Erlanger, who replaced her in Paris after covering the Middle East, added deeper layers.

The New York Times was hardly alone, but it was a good example. Complex stories need nuanced coverage orchestrated by thoughtful editors.

×

Iran in 2009 showed plainly what citizen journalism enthusiasts overlook. Anyone now can point a cell phone at drama in the streets and pass images on to millions. Speeches and sounds, what radio calls "actuality," come from all directions. But that is mostly ambience. When reporters are banned from covering complex stories firsthand, editors must piece together stories through the looking glass.

Much was made of how Tehran shut its borders and expelled correspondents. Yet that was hardly new, or rare. Scores of countries grant only limited visas to selected journalists – or none at all. A large percentage of foreign news-gathering can be done only from the outside.

Until Richard Nixon opened a hermetically sealed China in 1972, reporters peered into the Middle Kingdom from opaque windows in Hong Kong and Singapore. They did not learn much. With all the technology and travel these days, no country remains much of a mystery. But in such circumstances, it is very easy to get things wrong.

The trick to covering tightly sealed states is to look for unusual opportunities: national day festivities, sporting events, cultural tours. Even if minders dog a reporter's steps, any look in the door adds to a larger picture. Ghoulish as it may be, the best opportunities are when natural disasters strike.

For decades, I never managed to get into Algeria. Reporters were viewed with suspicion in any circumstance, and more so Americans with Semitic-sounding names. From the outside, Algeria seemed grim, with an authoritarian, faux-revolutionary junta whose overriding philosophy was hostility toward – and nostalgia for – France. Most Algerians I knew were migrant workers and dour diplomats.

When an earthquake shook Algeria in 2003, all comers were welcome. I was stunned at how much I admired the place. True, the leadership was as it looked from the outside: hard-line, suspicious, and defensive. But the people were different. Like Cubans, they told bitter jokes about the government; everyone seemed to know how far they could go. They cared deeply for family and friends. Unfailingly, they displayed elaborate generosity to a stranger.

My driver and I spent hours in Algiers sidewalk coffee shops discussing with his pals fine points of French literature and American politics. In the countryside, villagers lavished Islamic courtesy on foreigners they had been taught to mistrust.

One brief visit proves little on the grand scale. But as a reporter and also as an editor, I had formed a strong impression of a place I had never seen. And it was wrong. If I needed any further example of why exposure to the real world was crucial for gatekeepers, this was it.

×

A weakened bond between editors and reporters, the basis of so much past work, is among the great losses in 21st century journalism. Working relationships can come only over time. Reporters must earn their editors' respect. If editors are worthy of their jobs, they will reciprocate.

Smart correspondents make this their first priority whether they answer to a single foreign editor or a series of people who handle their copy. They recheck facts to dead certainty and are careful to point out what might not be clear. Their dispatches are clean, crisp, and solidly sourced. They stand their ground, but also listen to reason and swallow the urge to grumble.

Reporters must understand that editors, even incompetent ones, are higher up the pay scale. Bill Claiborne, who retired years ago from the *Washington Post,* offers timeless advice: a good correspondent is self-starting and low-maintenance.

The symbiosis between reporter and editor is particularly important when it comes to naming names. Many news executives hate anonymity because it invites public criticism. True enough, anonymous sources can be a lazy way to cut corners. In orderly societies, people with a viewpoint to sell like hiding behind anonymity when it suits their purpose. Like people who email comments on the news, they can heap slime on others without having the courage to add their names. But in much of the world, naming sources in a story can get them killed.

Time and again, when I interview an official who expects to be named I get the party line. If I can establish trust and assure anonymity, that same person says something diametrically opposed. Using unnamed sources, for instance, I was able to expose the government-backed death squads behind Argentina's dirty war. Every correspondent has a list of other examples. Watergate is a classic example — and the mysterious source, Deep Throat, only risked losing his job.

It all comes down to trust. A wise editor learns who will use anonymous sources responsibly and who might not. For this aspect alone, we need good gatekeepers as much as we need reporters worthy of being let through their gates.

Talk
Less,
Listen
More

chapter five

Try this as an experiment. Interview someone who is authoritative and articulate on a subject you care about. Afterward, play back the tape. Most likely, you will want to shoot yourself for rabbiting on when your expert is trying to get some wisdom in edgewise. Don't worry. That is common to all reporters, and we hate ourselves for it.

"The temptation to talk over your interviews is a terrible thing," Steven Erlanger of *The New York Times* told me before I interrupted him. A glance at his copy shows how much he absorbs by letting his sources tell the story. "You have to learn to listen," he said. "Silence contains a lot of information. Some of the best quotes come from silence. Let someone else fill it in."

Ed Cody of the *Washington Post* puts it more simply: "Shut the fuck up and listen."

The interview is fundamental to journalism, the best way to bring a source to life. Done right, it can provide far more information than your subject intends, with rich nonverbal detail that helps to gauge the weight of spoken words. You can learn from the weaves and dodges. At the beginning, you need to talk some to prime the pump and make your subject comfortable. Later, by not butting in, you offer no escape from hard questions.

Most interviews are simply grist for a larger story. Questions can be fragmented, only mildly coherent, and, if it serves a purpose, even dopey-sounding when read in transcript. Print reporters needle at times and wheedle at others. Nothing says they can't mumble. This is sausage-making, attractive only when the product emerges. The idea is to dig out fresh information and collect quotes that rarely run longer than 50 words.

Interviews to be printed verbatim take advance planning, with tightly worded questions leading toward specific points. Magazines such as *Der Spiegel* in Germany make a specialty of long Q & A exchanges taken straight off the recorder. Journalists come armed with substantial files of background, ready to nail inconsistencies and block off flights into extraneous territory.

Whatever the purpose, the main points are the same.

Jacqueline Sharkey takes the art of interviewing to a science. She has a few basic rules. Come prepared, with questions ready. Research your subject's politics and past remarks. The background helps direct your probing and also signals – importantly – that you have done your homework. Be respectful even if the guy is a mass murderer. He is a source not a potential brother-in-law. But mostly, listen.

"Silence is a wonderful interview technique," Sharkey says. "People are uncomfortable with it. I just sit there and look at them. Sometimes a minute or two will go by, and then they fill in the silence. That's usually when the most revealing things come out, things they would not have said. The mistake many young reporters make is that they also feel uncomfortable, and they talk too much."

It is not just young reporters. Jon Lee Anderson of *The New Yorker* sometimes cringes when he reviews tapes. "Half of it is me talking," he said. Busy people with much to say resent wasting their time. If they think you are not up to the subject, they are likely to patronize you and then clam up. But don't debate them or try to impress them with how much you know. Use your own knowledge to draw them out or jog their memories if they seem to be over-looking some important aspect.

A reverse technique, if you can pull it off, is what John Kifner of *The New York Times,* calls his dumb-schmuck approach. He listens wide-eyed and rapt, inspiring his sub-ject to get into tactical details he might not otherwise reveal to someone more expert. And then a different Kifner emerges to fire off sharp, specific questions.

Recording interviews is important. That ensures accurate lengthy quotes and settles future arguments about what was said. Still, always take careful notes. A pesky corollary of Murphy's Law is that the more interesting the interview, the more likely batteries will go flat. Many people shy away from recorders; some get aggressive about it. You may decide not to dampen a mood. Or you may not have time to mess around. Train yourself to write fast, with a sort of shorthand that you can read later on.

Learn what you can about body language, not just the basic folded-arms stuff but sophisticated indicators like breath rhythms, eyelid flutter rates, and jaw tension. Carefully read, these subtle clues can reveal dissimulation, even when sources are lying to themselves.

Once I helped Barry Goodfield, a psychotherapist friend who was hired to counsel Eastern European cabinet members on how to deal with the press. He videotaped interviews to catch what he calls unconscious nonverbal leaks. We learned more from what they didn't say — by the ways in which they didn't say it — than by their guarded spoken words. One minister heaped praise on a neighbor state. But he unconsciously kicked the air whenever he named it, foreshadowing fresh border tension.

Relaxed conversations can be better than interviews. Traveling with aid workers or military units usually offers long hours of down time, often with someone's tongue-lubricating flask. (Always bring one of your own.) Be wary of producing a pencil, let alone a microphone. But listen. If a particular quote or a chunk of information stands out, ask later for permission to use it. At the least, you will have valuable background insight.

Avoid phone interviews unless there is no choice. They save time, of course. But they give no sense of nonverbal language and physical setting. Subjects can't lean over to grab the document they suddenly decide to give you or summon an aide to brief you in detail. You'll want to notice that copy of *Mein Kampf* or the stuffed cheetah. Also, you want to develop sources. Someone who remembers your visit will take your calls in the future.

Email is fine to check a fact or clarify a point. For inter-views, it is a lazy copout. It gives subjects total control, allowing them to answer questions you don't ask and ignore ones you do. If you email a complex background question, you will likely provoke a stab at the delete key.

×

In television, interviews are often as much for theater as they are for eliciting information. On camera, you can seldom shut up and listen. Scarce airtime allows no rambling. Ratings demand articulate journalists with trademark looks and personalities. Yet when the questioner gets as much airtime as the subject, the interview itself can over-shadow what it is about.

This is a particular problem with American television. Brand-ers push individuals, who end up looming larger than the stories they cover. The result, often distracting, can border on clownish. When people who cover real news are identified with specific points of view — on immigration, for instance — their authority quickly wanes.

Even measured old hands can stray too far into the side-lights, missing the bigger story. American viewers have come to expect this. In other societies, it can cause doors to slam shut. A case in point was Lesley Stahl's non-interview for *60 Minutes* with French President Nicolas Sarkozy in October 2007.

Jacques Chirac had just left office after a long chill over Iraq, and George W. Bush wanted more French support. Sarkozy was about to visit the White House. He needed Washington behind him as he jockeyed within the European Union and in the wider world. Yet, like Chirac, he insisted on France's right to disagree. Probing questions would have cast light on a crucial alliance.

The segment title, "Sarko the American," set the tone: tell us about you, such as, what do you think about us? The subtitle might have been: tell a foreign TV reporter if you plan to divorce the beloved wife who dimmed your triumph and humiliated you by running off with another man. In 13 minutes, we saw only banter, canned background, and a flash of Sarzkoy's well-known prickliness.

Footage of the pre-interview setup showed Sarkozy railing

at an aide for scheduling a TV interview into his crowded schedule. "Imbecile," he said. Stahl admonished him. "But, sir, this is what the public, the American people are gonna see." He sneered briefly, seemingly ready to suggest where that public could go, but then held a frozen smile. Stahl made calm-down gestures, condescending under the circumstances. Then the interview started.

After some remarks about Sarkozy's Hungarian father and France's 35-hour work week, Stahl got to the point: "Since we've been here, it seems that every day we're hearing another story about your wife. What's going on?"

"If I had something to say something about Cecilia," Sarkozy replied through the wooden smile, "I would certainly not do so here."

That would have been a good time to switch to Iraq, Afghanistan, or Crawford, Texas. Stahl persisted: "But there's a great mystery. Everyone's asking. Even your press secretary was asked at the briefing."

As he yanked out his earpiece and stood up to go, Sarkozy said, "Well, he was quite right to make no comment. And no comment. *Merci.*"

In the piece that aired, Sarkozy spoke only a few other sentences. Some friendly chat was added from a short flight Stahl had taken earlier with him. But since he had refused a mike, it was mostly noise.

Obviously enough, television also provides plenty of substance. Cameras allow a unique opportunity for people to take their own measure of leaders who are reshaping their world. Crossing cultural bridges is far easier when television adds visual backdrops and close-up vignettes.

When you watch an interview, it should be quickly clear whether the purpose is an addition to the world's knowledge or a ratings boost. These are not mutually exclusive, but if forced to chose, favor the former. If you conduct one, try to forget that an audience is watching.

As one example, look carefully at how Christiane Amanpour interviews world leaders. If now a household fixture, she came up the hard way as a CNN reporter during the first Gulf War. Her plummy British-Persian inflection exudes authority, but what matters is her grasp of the issues and personalities that shape global events.

Or watch the BBC for a while, particularly its redoubtable *Newsnight*. It will be immediately plain why a good TV reporter need not pose or posture for the camera.

×

Radio is an ideal medium for interviews, with ample time and no visuals to overpower the simple sound of a subject's persona. The best reporters make it sound easy yet it is anything but. Sharp questions ferret out news, and softer ones sketch in background. Tactful interruptions are often necessary as engineers count the seconds.

When Hillary Clinton or the Dalai Lama is at the mike, introductions can be skipped. Otherwise, listeners need clues. The French method is unnerving. Subjects are addressed directly as if they've never heard of themselves: "You were born on the planet Krypton and are famous for your red and blue tight pants, funny cape, and penchant for telephone booths." But it works.

The best radio interviewers know when to let a subject ramble and when to break in for a sudden 90-degree turn. With a command of the subject, they can challenge false assertions and add the disconcerting details their subjects take pains to skirt. And looks do not matter. Every reporter has a good enough face for radio.

×

Dictators and shady characters tend to shun print reporters, who might grill them hard and shape the story by selecting quotes to cite. They prefer to talk directly into cameras or microphones. But even for broadcast reporters, getting to them often takes skill and perseverance.

Traditional news organizations have fractured into spinoffs and splinters. Bloggers and independent reporters have joined their ranks, intensifying the competition. Many high-profile people now set conditions. Some want to be paid. Too many editors comply, eager for bragging rights. News seldom emerges in such cases, but marketing departments are thrilled.

Journalists need to draw clear lines. Networks might send a car or cover out-of-pocket expenses. It is reasonable enough to take someone to lunch if that opens doors. But reporters should not pay for interviews under any circumstance. Nor should they let their subjects preview questions or review transcripts. If an interview is not an honest give-and-take, it is a media appearance.

Below the ranks of presidents and superstars, many interviews can be surprisingly easy to get. Ask and keep asking until time and place are fixed. Yet some are painfully difficult to arrange.

Most people like to talk, however much they may protest to the contrary, but many need to be courted. Years ago, Hugh Mulligan of AP scored a rare conversation with Vladimir Nabokov in Switzerland after a long exchange of letters, literary and witty, that amused the elusive writer. I took an easier route with Graham Greene; I cornered him at the Antibes market as he shopped for tomatoes.

Try to sidestep overprotective handlers. Fidel Castro once visited Burgundy wine country during a sensitive period; people were fleeing his island at a fast clip. He tried to answer my shouted questions, but Cuban and French security guards loomed in between. I waited until he finished a three-hour lunch, which I knew would be well lubricated with Chablis. Properly loaded, he barreled toward me, grinning broadly and knocking aside guards like so many bowling pins. I asked when he would be coming to visit the United States. "It's so close," he said, "maybe I'll go on a raft."

Often subjects want to know what you are after. That is reasonable as long as you give only general clues. Once seated, go wherever you can steer the conversation. If a subject declines to discuss personal affairs, let it go. American public figures live with prurient curiosity. But as Lesley Stahl saw in Paris, other cultures see things differently. Focus on what really matters. When you are satisfied with what you've got, try again at the end.

×

For most stories, good sources willing to talk are all over the place. You simply have to find them. And then shut up and listen. This takes resisting the temptation to play with our wondrous new toys.

In Darfur, Jerome Tubiana, a French ethnographer friend working with an aid agency, tried to help a visiting British reporter. He produced a *janjaweed* chieftain and offered to interpret, a rare opportunity for insight. The reporter declined. Instead, he spent his few hours in Darfur exchanging text messages with editors and friends. Later, aid workers found his website.

"We had big fun reading some of his heroic twits after seeing his performance in the field," Tubiana told me. "We diverged only on whether he was the archetypal 2009 journalist or an exception."

The jury is still out, but the signs are unsettling. Satellite links to home are only part of it. Most reporters now carry not only a notebook but also a sound recorder and a video camera. Each has a place. But one must be wary of using them all at once.

No one can listen carefully while stabbing at buttons and fussing with settings. When waiting for the right picture, you will miss a vital word or gesture. But worse is the inevitable impact on subjects. In Darfur, people are likely to stare mutely at your gadgetry, either overcome by curiosity or pondering whether to steal it. In Denmark, they are more prone to laugh at your awkward antics. Either way, do not expect much depth.

Reliable
Sources

chapter six

It is troubling how often we use that hoary phrase, "reliable sources," considering there is no such thing. "Usually reliable sources" is better; it allows for human error and human nature. But it sounds pretty awkward. In any case, there is always a hanging question: Was that source's information reliably transmitted?

Confirming facts is all the more important as journalism loosens its old strictures. "Crowdsourcing" can produce useful nuggets of information, but mobs generally miss the larger truth. And stopping to verify a story impedes the scramble to be first.

In 2010, Peter Tague tried an experiment with his Georgetown law students. He told them Chief Justice John Roberts was about to resign, but he would not reveal his source. And he asked them to keep the news confidential. By the time he explained he was messing with them to make a point, half an hour later, the story was everywhere.

Radar Online, a gossip site, picked up a student's Twitter alert and reported an "exclusive." It gave no reason but speculated on Roberts' health. Later, instead of retracting the report, it said Roberts had changed his mind. Meantime, Fox News and other major outlets had broadcast the story.

The crux of good reporting is an ability to handle sources: to choose them carefully, to absorb what each says, to factor in filters and caveats, and, finally, to mix and match them into a trustworthy package.

We have for years stood by a two-source guideline. If someone tells you something, and someone else confirms it, it is solid. Today, this is no guarantee. One accurate source is better than two sources who get it wrong. Spurious information now flies around so fast that a second source might be repeating, unwittingly and unconsciously, baseless hearsay.

The two-source rule was the basis for the *Washington Post* Watergate scoops that brought down Richard Nixon. A senior official, disgusted at what his bosses were up to, fed kernels of the story to Bob Woodward and Carl Bernstein. When any part of the big picture could be nailed down with a second unrelated source, it made the paper. After months of probing, enough pieces of the puzzle were fit together. The Administration collapsed.

If reporters and their readers are not careful, it also works the other way.

In 1955, Izzy Stone wrote in his wise little I.F. Stone's Weekly: "The main obstacle to the creation of a well-informed public is its own indifference." Publishing is a business not a Jeffersonian passion, he wrote. Making waves can be costly, he added, and too many journalists go along to get along in what has always been a conformist society.

Stone wrote: "One of our very best reporters, James Reston of *The New York Times,* put his finger on the vital point when he said that worse than suppression was the 'managing' of the news by government departments. But the news is 'managed' because the reporters and their editors let themselves be managed."

×

Nothing so dramatically illustrates manipulation of sources than the prelude to America's war in Iraq. The invasion and all that followed show with chilling clarity why the world so badly needs trained foreign correspondents committed to digging out truth.

After George W. Bush took power in 2001, he and Vice President Dick Cheney began building a case for toppling Saddam Hussein. Al Qaeda attacked America from Afghanistan, but they wanted a casus belli for invading Iraq. For that, they needed congressional and public support.

In a stage-managed news conference late in 2002, Bush painted Saddam as the mastermind behind Islamic terrorists. This bogus story line picked up momentum fast. Washington reporters favored high-level officials and politically motivated sources over lower-ranking insiders whose consciences prompted them to speak frankly. And editors shunted aside contradicting reports from the Middle East.

In 2007, Bill Moyers deconstructed this process in a 90-minute PBS report entitled *Buying the War* (www.pbs. org/moyers/journal/btw). No young journalist should be let out of the box before studying it. Citizens ought to be made to see it, eyes taped open a la Clockwork Orange, before they enter a voting booth.

Buying the War captured the mood after mysterious dark forces dared attack Americans on their own turf. As Bush spoke in the World Trade Center ruins, crowds chanted, "USA, USA," and made that curious woofing noise which heralds mob mentality. People wanted revenge and did not care against whom. Plainly, America needed eyes and ears out in a world it was about to reconfigure.

Allies and enemies alike understood the United States had to strike hard at the obvious culprits in Afghanistan. But Bush enlisted British Prime Minister Tony Blair to help make his case against Iraq. To justify invasion, envoys went abroad to find links between Saddam and al Qaeda. White House strategists added spin to intelligence reports.

Much was made of an alleged meeting in Prague between an al Qaeda operative, Mohammed Atta, and Iraqi agents. Correspondents who knew the characters were dubious. Iraq was a strictly secular state. Saddam and Osama Bin Laden hated one another.

Moyers questioned Bob Simon of CBS, who had gone to Prague to investigate supposed links. Simon had spent decades in the Middle East and was hardly soft on Saddam. He was captured by Iraqis during the first Gulf War and brutalized for 40 days.

"Saddam, as most tyrants, was a total control freak," Simon said. "He wanted total control of his regime ... his country. And to introduce a wild card like al Qaeda in any sense was just something he would not do. So I just didn't believe it for an instant."

Washington reporters swallow such "absurdity," Simon said,

because they work in a bubble, with the same familiar top-
level sources. "When the Washington press corps travels,
it travels with the president or the secretary of state,
whereas we who have spent weeks just walking the streets
of Baghdad ... were just scratching our heads."

In Washington, meantime, Cheney cited on NBC's *Meet the
Press* "public knowledge" that Saddam was seeking tubes
to build a centrifuge for enhancing low-grade uranium into
the highly enriched core of a nuclear bomb. On morning
television, Condoleezza Rice delivered a White House
speech writer's show-stopper line: "We don't want the
smoking gun to be a mushroom-shaped cloud." Newspapers quoted this the next morning. Bush adopted it as an
unchallenged mantra.

Simon laughed at the episode. "Remarkable," he told Moyers.
"You leak a story, and then you quote the story. I mean,
that's a remarkable thing to do." Here was the perfect
perversion of the multi-source rule.

The administration declared unequivocally that Saddam hid
nuclear, chemical, and biological weapons. Reporters in
Iraq were skeptical. They followed U.N. inspectors whose
methodical searching had found nothing. Teams raced off
without warning, often suddenly changing direction, to
ensure Iraqis hid no evidence before they arrived. In
Washington, however, the press corps trusted their reliable
sources to support the case for war.

As war clouds gathered, Charles Hanley of AP went to
Baghdad to monitor the monitors. Hanley is as solid a
reporter as the profession produces. He won a Pulitzer
for uncovering a civilian massacre by U.S. troops in Korea;
the Pentagon had covered it up for half a century. Just
before Colin Powell made his case to the U.N. Security
Council, Hanley wrote a detailed piece pointing out the
flaws in his facts. For instance, Powell said Iraqis put a roof
over one facility to hide it from satellites. He neglected
to say that inspectors had crawled all over the site, under
the roof, and found nothing. AP editors killed the story.

Hanley told Moyers:

"The media just continued on this path of reporting. 'Well, the Bush administration alleges that there are WMD,' and never really stopped and said, 'It doesn't look like there are. There's no evidence.' That should have been the second sentence in any story about the allegations of WMD. The second sentence should have been: 'But they did not present any evidence to back this up.'"

×

Looking back, Moyers' documentary is important not only for what it revealed in such irrefutable detail but also for the impact it failed to have on an apathetic public. It is a classic example for the study of sourcing, a clarion call for us all to do better. Yet the same flawed processes remain in place today. And now there are even fewer foreign correspondents to counter them.

Columnists who championed the war and mocked those who questioned it declined to speak with Moyers. Most gave excuses, but Charles Krauthammer of the Washington Post simply ignored requests to appear. Only Peter Beinart, who in 2002 was the 28-year-old wunderkind editor of the *New Republic,* accepted and admitted he had gotten it wrong.

Beinart had never been to Iraq, he said, but he had his sources. The exchange went like this:

BILL MOYERS: How do you get the information that enables you to reach the conclusion that you draw as a political journalist?

PETER BEINART: Well, I was doing mostly, for a large part it was reading, reading the statements and the things that people said. I was not a beat reporter. I was editing a magazine and writing a column. So I was not doing a lot of primary reporting. But what I was doing was

a lot of reading of other people's reporting
and reading of what officials were saying.

BILL MOYERS: If we journalists get it wrong on
the facts what is there to be right about?

PETER BEINART: Well I think that's a good
point, but the argument in the fall of 2002
was not mostly about the facts; it was about a
whole series of ideas about what would happen
if we invaded.

Moyers' exchange with Bob Simon is revealing. He showed
a snippet from *60 Minutes* in December 2002 in which Simon
says, "It's not the first time a president has mounted a
sales campaign to sell a war."

Then Moyers added: "There was little appetite inside the
networks for taking on a popular, wartime president. So
Simon decided to wrap his story inside a more benign
account of how the White House was marketing the war."

The Selling the War transcript reads:

BOB SIMON: I think we all felt from the beginning that to deal with a subject as explosive
as this, we should keep it in a way almost
light. If that doesn't seem ridiculous.

BILL MOYERS: Going to war, almost light.

BOB SIMON: Not to present it as a frontal
attack on the Administration's claims. Which
would have been not only premature, but we
didn't have the ammunition to do it at the
time. We did not know then that there were no
weapons of mass destruction in Iraq. We only
knew that the connection the Administration
was making between Saddam and Al Qaeda was
very tenuous at best and that the argument it
was making over the aluminum tubes seemed

highly dubious. We knew these things. And
therefore we could present the Madison Avenue
campaign on these things, which was a sort of
softer, less confrontational way of doing it.

BILL MOYERS: Did you go to any of the brass at
CBS, even at 60 MINUTES, and say, "Look, we
gotta dig deeper. We gotta connect the dots.
This isn't right."

BOB SIMON: No, in all honesty, with a thousand
mea culpas, I've done a few stories in Iraq.
But, nope, I don't think we followed up on this.

Television, as usually happens, followed the newspapers,
notably *The New York Times*. Judith Miller, whose string of
stories did much to sell the war, also declined to appear
in the documentary. Forced to leave the *Times* with only
a tepid mea culpa, Miller later admitted she was wrong. Her
sources had misled her, she said. What is a reporter to do?

×

The heroes of Moyers' piece are Jonathan Landay and
Warren Strobel, reporters for Knight Ridder Newspapers,
and their bureau chief, John Walcott. Their hard digging
should have ranked them with Woodward, Bernstein, and
Ben Bradlee in journalism history. Instead, they amount
to a footnote. Knight Ridder has since been bought up,
dismantled, and partly subsumed by McClatchy.

Landay took time to examine U.N. inspectors' reports, all
online, and he went to the Iraq Nuclear Verification Office.
So he was surprised when Cheney told a veterans' group
that Iraq would soon have nuclear weapons.

JONATHAN LANDAY: I looked at that and I said,
"What is he talking about?" Because, to develop a nuclear weapon you need specific infrastructure and in particular the way the Iraqis
were trying to produce a nuclear weapon was

through enrichment of uranium. Now, you need tens of thousands of machines called centrifuges to produce highly enriched uranium for a nuclear weapon. You've gotta house those in a fairly big place, and you've gotta provide a huge amount of power to this facility. Could he really have done it with all of these eyes on his country?

DICK CHENEY: (Speech to the VFW 8/26/02) But we now know that Saddam has resumed his efforts to acquire nuclear weapons.

JONATHAN LANDAY: So, when Cheney said that, I got on the phone to people, and one person said to me - somebody who watched proliferation as their job - said, "The Vice President is lying."

But none of Knight Ridder's 32 dailies circulated in New York or Washington. In the *Washington Post,* Joby Warrick wrote a tough piece questioning the evidence. It ran on page 18 with no impact.

Press critic Howard Kurtz did the math. Between August 2002 and March 2003 the *Post* ran 140 front-page pieces that made the case for war, mostly quoting the White House or the Pentagon. Only a few raised questions. "Those stories, and some reporters worked hard on them, had a harder time getting on the front page," Kurtz said. "Why? Because they weren't definitive."

So Knight Ridder, with papers in places like Akron and Wichita and San Jose, was essentially alone in going to those usually reliable sources behind the scenes.

"Our readers ... aren't the people who send other people's kids to war." Walcott said. "They're the people who were sent to war, and we felt an obligation to explain why. We were determined to scrutinize the Administration's case for war as closely as possible."

Strobel added:

"When you're talking to the working grunts, you know, uniform military officers, intelligence professionals, professional diplomats, those people are more likely than not – not always, of course, but more likely than not – to tell you some version of the truth, and to be knowledgeable about what they're talking about when it comes to terrorism or the Middle East, things like that."

In the end, Knight Ridder came up with more than a dozen sources who asserted the administration's case was bunk, and they were eager to explain why. Even if no one was listening, Deep Throats were talking. The reason was no different than it was with Watergate.

"There are people within the U.S. government who object when they perceive that their government isn't being straight with the people," Landay said. "And when they perceive that an administration is veering away from the principles on which this country was built, they become more ready to talk about things that perhaps they ordinarily shouldn't.

×

The lesson here is hardly only about the United States or stories of world-shaping magnitude. In almost every human situation, some people lie outright or distort reality for their own benefit. A reporter's job is to find others who try hard to tell the truth and do the right thing. For this, two sources are seldom close to enough.Jacqueline Sharkey has a variation on that Ronald Reagan caution, trust but verify. Hers is, Don't trust– and verify until you are blue in the face. This applies not only to sources' statements but also to those ubiquitous statistics, charts, and studies given to support a case.

Numbers are famously misleading, no matter how official or authoritative their origin. Surveys and polls are only indicators, not necessarily useful ones.

Reporters must be clear when using statistics, polling results, or financial figures. Always identify the source and add, if possible, the methods used. If other authoritative numbers suggest a different picture, say so.

Crowd estimates are especially tricky. A million-man march falls flat if only tens of thousands show up. But even a fraction of a million can be a hell of a crowd, and a moving mass is hard to count. Organizers tend to add a zero or two. Detractors take zeros away. Police officials are the usual source. But their numbers can be wildly wrong, particularly if the crowd is protesting authority.

Economic statistics are routinely cooked, stacked to fortify a particular purpose. During 2009, the euro collapsed when Greece's reserves suddenly came up far shorter than anyone expected. *The New York Times* reported that Goldman Sachs had helped Greek authorities disguise imbalances with deft sleights of hand.

With the best of intentions, international agencies can be far off the mark. United Nations statistics are based on questionable and uneven data from member states. And some things are simply uncountable. For instance, how do you quantify poverty? By the widely used World Bank measure, people earning less than $2 a day are poor. At less than $1.20 a day, they are extremely poor. A family in rural India can live on that. In the suburbs of Berlin or Paris, a daily euro goes a very short way.

People who want to do more than comfort their own prejudices and misconceptions can do their own sourcing, just as good reporters do. This takes triangulation, a simple process of suspending belief until enough confirming sources give it a clear ring of truth.

Start by discarding obvious agitprop, much of which is pathetically evident.

Recently, a smart friend whose field is analyzing how humans think asked my opinion about a chain-linked story someone had sent him. It began: "AP–WASHINGTON D.C. — In a move certain to fuel the debate over Obama's qualifications for the presidency, the "Americans for Freedom of Information" has Released copies of President Obama's college transcripts from Occidental College."

Anyone who reads news could have dismissed that out of hand on form alone: that is not how AP does datelines. AP's stories, whatever their strengths or weaknesses, are written and edited by literate people according to specific style. "Obama" is not how it would identify a head of state on first reference. And it is hardly news that some unknown group "Releases" a report.

But the howler is the fourth paragraph, the buried lead, which says Justice Antonin Scalia announced the Supreme Court would hear arguments concerning Obama's eligibility to be president. We most likely would have heard at least one confirming report elsewhere. For a final chuckle, it was dated April 1.

This was sent to my friend by a radio personality with a large following. If professionals can be taken in by a transparent hoax about America's own chief executive, imagine what circulates from little-known places abroad.

If your original source is a news outlet you have learned to trust, so much the better. Google and Yahoo don't count. They only relay others' reporting. Wise readers hold information in a temporary memory cache — or better yet, write it down— until other sources solidify it. For reporters who assemble raw bits of information, the process is more complex. But the principle is the same. The trick is to be sure that a confirming source is not simply an echo bounced back from someone who has it wrong.

Fair and Kinderspiel

chapter seven

When left-wing terrorists began targeting businessmen in Argentina, Oscar Serrat of The Associated Press hurried to a remote Pampas crossroads where kidnappers had dumped a prominent executive. He watched police examine bullet exit wounds on the cold body, and he filed a story. Not long after he returned to the bureau, the phone rang.

You say this man is dead, a New York editor barked down the line. What's the source?

Serrat explained that he had seen an exceedingly dead corpse. He was a skilled reporter, an Argentine then still unhindered by excess familiarity with news agency ways.

You need a source, the editor said.

Serrat told me about this later. "You mean," he fumed, "I'm supposed to go up a policeman, point to the dead guy, and ask if he's dead? He'll think I'm an idiot."

Yes, I agreed. But, silly as it was, that was the rule. The victim could be ground up in a wood chipper and discovered after three weeks. You still needed some variation of "police said."

This was in the 1970s when journalistic style demanded copious amounts of such attribution, no matter what the story. And there was a parallel. If a story made an assertion, editors generally demanded someone to express an opposing view. If some Nobel-winning geographer said the world was round, it would not have surprised me if the desk wanted some think-tank doofus to insist it was pear-shaped.

Nate Polowetzky, AP foreign editor, used to laugh off the extremes as kinderspiel. In Yiddish, a kid's game.

There was a purpose for those rules then; there still is. Reporters should quote authoritative sources. When an assertion can be argued, legitimate questions belong in the story. But like most rules, they come with corollaries.

After years of covering a region, or a subject, reporters are often more qualified than the experts they interview. Their dispatches need attributed quotes to support the points they make. Legitimate opposing views are crucial.

But experienced reporters can, in the end, depict situations as they know them to be. Stories that leave uninformed readers to make up their minds on complex issues add little to a news report.

During the 1970s, Wes Gallagher was AP general manager and a leading influence on how the American press covered news at home and abroad. Gallagher, the last AP chief executive who had been a foreign correspondent, had covered World War II and its aftermath in Europe.

Though known for rapid arbitrary decisions, Gallagher also kept an open mind. When Peter Arnett described U.S. troops looting a Vietnamese village they had captured, he tried to kill the story. "GI's don't loot," he declared. And, naturally, military spokes-men denied it. But the foreign desk rebelled. Gallagher backed down, deciding to support his man on the spot.

After he retired, senior editors invited their old boss to drop in for an after-work discussion on the evolving news business. He stunned them by ridiculing kinderspiel in political reporting.

Pertinent sourcing and substantive counter arguments were essential to stories, he said. But if one party outlined a posi-tion based on facts, he asked, why include the other party's ritual naysaying? Of course, the opposition would oppose. Instead, it was better to wait until the other side had its own fact-based position.

This should apply to all types of stories, he said. Competent reporters who do their job well should be free to let facts guide readers. Giving equal weight to opposing viewpoints simply con-fuses people who don't have the background to decide which is closer to reality.

Kinderspiel is still with us in multiple forms.

Often it is a distorting hedge against reaction from readers. In one such case, an AP reporter described how a Palestinian woman died in childbirth in a car that was blocked at a checkpoint out of Gaza. The desk added to the lead paragraph a denial from an

Israeli spokesman in Jerusalem who could not possibly have known the facts.

On a far larger scale, kinderspiel is why the world took so long to acknowledge climate change. Back in the 1980s, scientists from around the world examined evidence and sounded the alarm. Reporters who noticed these early warnings tempered them with views from the other side.

At first, this was understandable enough. We've been living with our climate for a long time, and it seems pretty far-fetched that CO2 emissions could change it. But as time went on, alarms grew louder, backed by evidence. The Intergovernmental Panel on Climate Change issued periodic reports, with mounting irre-futable data. Before long, anyone who looked could see the evidence firsthand.

As data piled up, oil companies and others with an interest in preserving status quo – multiple billions of dollars hung in the balance – issued ever-louder denials. Far too often, news outlets gave them equal space. Partly, the problem was that some edi-tors provoke by purposely countering perceived beliefs. But more, too few reporters took the trouble to study the facts for themselves.

Late in 2009, as world leaders headed toward Copenhagen to draft a treaty to thwart climate change, a story broke about how a group of scientists had given short shrift to colleagues who questioned majority conclusions. Emails were suppressed, and data was stuck in the drawer.

On a global scale, this changed nothing. As Paul Krugman wrote in *The New York Times*, it proved only that scientists are human. But the story received such sustained attention that it cast doubt on 20 years of hard science by thousands of specialists across the world. Balance is one thing; kinderspiel is another.

Journalists cannot be experts in everything. Instead, they should be experts in experts. That requires evaluating sources' competence, ferreting out hidden interests, and then looking hard for observable facts. In this case, any glacier, coral reef,

or desert suggested which side of the argument carried
more weight.

×

The basic rules are simple enough: If a story demands a
balancing counterpoint, be sure it is there. Governments,
businesses, and individuals all have a right to reply if the
story directly concerns them. However damning a story
might seem, mitigating circumstances might alter the
picture. In any case, it is only right to hear them out.

A reporter's job is to try hard for comment. If autho-
rized spokespeople choose to stonewall, or if the only
access to them is by sending an email to an anonymous
"media inquiries" address, at least the effort was made.

The tricky part is the wording and placement of their
comment. A reporter's role is to guide the uninformed.
That means being fair in every instance. Balance is harder
to pin down. A ritual "on the one hand this and the other
hand that" usually skews reality.

In trustworthy journalism, reporters do not express
opinions in news reports. European styles can stray far
from the straitlaced "just the facts, ma'am" American
approach. Still, stories must follow the facts however
they might fit with the writer's or editor's own prejudices.
False balance misleads as much as getting the facts wrong.

Readers need clues. Governments and corporations lie; it
is in the nature of things. Smart officials and executives
shelter behind the friendlier synonym, spin. When con-
sciously done, as it almost always is, that is still lying. The
safe approach of simply giving two, or three, sides of the
story is not good enough.

Gulf War One was a revealing study of kinderspiel. In
August 1990, Saddam Hussein's troops swarmed into Kuwait,
sealing off the coastal emirate. During the run-up to
invasion early in 1991, the closest anyone could get was

the Saudi border town of Khafji, 100 miles from Kuwait City. And that took some doing.

American and coalition forces set up headquarters in the Saudi capital, Riyadh. A U.S. Joint Information Bureau (JIB) organized a daily news conference for a multinational mob of journalists. Unlike the Five O'clock Follies in Vietnam, these circus acts were televised live to American homes. Generals played to the public. Flashy gun-camera footage from attacking jets made death and suffering down below look like a simple video game.

When reporters asked hard questions, some people back home demanded they be banned from their own news briefings because they disrespected officers who were trying to communicate with Americans whose families were at war.

Many of us based at the International Hotel in Dhahran, Saudi Arabia, down the coast from Khafji and closer to the action. Riyadh briefings were relayed by closed-circuit TV, and we watched in silence. As Tony Clifton of *Newsweek* grumbled, "In Vietnam, at least they lied to us in person."

Access was a nightmare. Vietnam taught the U.S. military how to shape the message and market war. Reporters who roam freely across undefined battlefields see far too much reality. So the JIB in Dhahran organized small pools to selected sites. Officers chose from among a clamoring horde of supplicants, who tried to stay in their good graces. Some of us made "unilateral" forays wherever we could skirt U.S. and Saudi roadblocks, but any troops we quoted were tracked down and punished.

Unlike the generals, American news executives ignored those Vietnam lessons. Many simply wanted dramatic footage of exploding ordnance — even in practice — along with quotes from grunts in uniform. Rather than resist the pool system together, journalists fought among themselves for a spot.

News organizations sent some seasoned hands to cover the war. They also sent untried young reporters, some who had never crossed a border, who wrote pool reports for everyone else. As a result, it was the military's show.

One afternoon, an AP photographer back from a pool to the Marines' forward base showed me pictures of long silver canisters slung under the wings of Harrier aircraft. I hurried over to the Marine spokesman, a friendly captain.

"I know you can't confirm or deny," I told him, "but smile if you're using napalm." He grinned. The U.S. command had denied dropping napalm on Iraq, still sensitive from criticism during the Vietnam War.

I asked my AP colleague in Riyadh to tell the Marine commander what we knew and to get comment. This happened to be Richard Pyle, a military maven who had been AP bureau chief in Saigon. The general, when pinned down by Pyle's precise questions, admitted napalm was used. But he said it was only against gun emplacements, not troops.

The captain rolled his eyes when I read him the general's quote. He asked if I had ever seen what happens to gunners when a bunker is hit by flaming jellied gasoline that sucks away oxygen. I had. My dispatch reported the use of napalm, previously denied, and explained its effects. Official comment came across as flimflam.

That brief war was a textbook case of how young journalists learn from old hands and vice versa. Washington-based reporters knew far more than foreign correspondents about Pentagon intricacies and new hardware. Tech-savvy colleagues, fresh from home, taught us much about computer wizardry, still in its early stages. We helped some avoid blowing themselves to bits by stepping on mines.

But kinderspiel is a tough game to avoid.

Late at night after the napalm story moved, a young woman from a North Carolina television station banged on my hotel room door. How, she demanded, could I write about napalm if I wasn't in the pool? How, I asked, could she not have told us about napalm if she was in the pool?

"They said they use that stuff only against matériel, not personnel," she replied, repeating the official dodge, complete with the jargon.

×

As stringers and long-distance guesswork replace trained correspondents, the ability to obfuscate increases dramatically. Plenty of reporters do fine from the start and get steadily better. But readers and viewers have no way to know which is which. Global newsgathering needs to rest on a solid and essentially reliable base, with old hands to season new ones.

When I first started out, smugly confident with a journalism degree and experience on the AP World Desk, I covered an African summit in Kinshasa. President Kenneth Kaunda of Zambia called the British prime minister a traitor, and I rushed to the telex to bash out an urgent story. In those early days of gentlemanly North – South geopolitics, this was strong stuff.

But Kaunda had said trader, not traitor, an accurate enough description for a European leader dealing with Africa. My Arizona-tuned ear misheard the inflection, and I had not stopped to think. Why would Kaunda call Harold Wilson a traitor? Answer: He wouldn't, and he didn't.

That was a lesson I never forgot. When you quote people, get their words accurately. Do not guess. Do not approximate from memory. If you are not sure of an exact quote, paraphrase. If you are not certain of what you heard, check it again. And it is equally important is get the sense right. If it sounds wrong, it probably is. If not, then fit it into a broader context.

People with important things to say can be surprisingly

inarticulate. People with something to sell, or hide, can lie shamelessly with a straight face. A stenographer's job is to take down dictation and pass it along. A reporter's job is different.

As Oscar Serrat knew instinctively at the Argentina crime scene, what matters most is witnessing the story first-hand and describing reality without unnecessary filters to fuzzy the facts or state the obvious. This, of course, requires a reporter's presence at the story.

"GroundTruth"

chapter eight

For NASA, ground truth is the spot where a satellite pin-point on the map intersects with a measurement made on the ground by an actual human being. Whatever instruments say, NASA believes, someone has to be there to check. When Charles Sennott designed the Web-based news agency, GlobalPost (www.globalpost.com), he wrote a correspondents' field guide, GroundTruth. Its first rule is simple enough: Be there.

This gets to the heart of any serious discussion of the "media." How newspapers survive in print is not the issue. What other forms news outlets take is mostly a business matter. Yes, much of the media is tendentious, meant more to shock, amuse, and comfort prejudices than to impart reliable information about the world. None of that changes the nature of good reporting. In the end, it all comes back to the essence: Be there.

Sennott put together a team of young people starting out, established freelancers, and veteran correspondents with extra time on their hands. They each earn a basic minimum, which they supplement with other strings or jobs unrelated to journalism. GlobalPost shares some reporting expenses with other outlets. Revenue comes from news-papers and broadcasters that use GP like AP. It is free online, but a small fee buys premium "content." (Try to avoid that word in a job interview with any old pro.)

GlobalPost is a professional operation, like the best of experimental new ventures. As star correspondent for the Boston Globe, Sennott learned to do it right. He hires reporters who live in the places they write about, who speak the languages and know the cultures. His small staff of editors in Boston rides herd, shaping eager neophytes into experienced hands.

In brief, GroundTruth comes down to seven key points:

Be there.
Stay safe.
Listen.
Be fair and accurate.
Be honest.
Stick to deadlines and stay in touch.
Tell great stories.
—

If some of these points seem obvious, there is much to say about each. "Stay safe" is no less important than "Be there," and it seems to get harder by the year. The International News Safety Institute in London (www.newssafety. org) tallies more than 1,000 journalists, translators, and fixers killed over the past decade. Countless others have been held hostage, imprisoned, wounded, or injured. Some were targeted for stories they wrote. Others were in the wrong place at the wrong time.

Professional groups have written volumes of practical advice. I refer to some in Chapter 11 and list others in the Appendix. Most recommend hostile environment training, which teaches things like first aid, driving techniques, dealing with roadblocks, and surviving captivity. That helps, but there is much more to it.

"Listen" is crucial for any reporter anywhere. Sennott says it well: "We believe strongly that the greatest correspondents hear as many sides of an issue as possible before they begin writing or produce multimedia. The most memorable stories are the ones that surprise us, that contravene our preconceptions. And we believe those stories come from listening carefully to the community you are covering. They come from being fair and reporting without bias."

News is too often shaped by politicians, officials, and diplomats, Sennott continues. "But the best reporting is the kind of reporting that comes up from the street that includes the voices of the people who stand to be affected by the decisions of the powerful."

x

The others may be self-evident, but "Be honest" touches on the points that have earned correspondents respect and trust over generations. Some of these are clear-cut and dead obvious: Don't make up quotes or facts, doctor images, or plagiarize. Some misguided editors may condone transgressions or even urge you to juice up a story.

Resist; this is wrong.

But there is more to being honest.

Some governments do not differentiate between journalist and spy. A few, like Iran's, keep reporters in line by singling out vulnerable ones for harsh punishment. Journalists should declare themselves, seek accreditation, and keep their visas current. Enterprising correspondents might choose to evade authorities to reach an otherwise inaccessible story. This is dangerous ground, and experience is vital. You have to know the rules before deciding to break them.

Shun gifts, paid expenses, or free flights. It is not enough to accept something on the understanding that it will not affect the story. Like so many rules, this can get fuzzy. Years ago, *Newsweek* told its correspondents not to take anything they could not consume in one day. One decided to keep a case of Cognac on the grounds that he could consume it all if he put his mind to it.

Perceptions matter on a large scale, even if the point might be missed in any one circumstance. Back in 1968, President Mobutu invited the Kinshasa press corps on a flight to the far end of the Congo. (Later, we learned, he was transferring captured mercenaries to a detention camp and wanted us out of town.) An aide handed each of us a thick envelope with expense money. Following AP rules, I gave mine back. His wide smile suggested he was unlikely to inform his superiors, and my gesture was lost. But still.

×

"Be honest" is as important a rule for news executives as it is for reporters. Yet far too many of them sacrifice honesty for expediency, thus decimating media credibility. Ventures such as GlobalPost, and editors like Sennott, attempt to get back to journalism's basic values.

Tom Fenton discussed these points in a book he called Bad

News. He worked for CBS, covering global news for 40 years. But if you change the letters and add in newspaper nameplates, you see a broader picture.

He wrote:

The London Bureau of CBS News ... doesn't do much reporting anymore. What it does is called packaging. We take in pictures shot by people we do not know, and wrap them in facts gathered by anonymous employees in news agencies owned by others. Call it the news media's version of outsourcing. All the television networks now do most of their 'reporting' this way, to save money on old-fashioned shoe-leather reporting by full-time correspondents. And as a result, the networks can no longer vouch for much of the foreign news they put on the air. Just as Dan Rather did so disastrously with those dodgy Bush memos that hastened the end of his career as anchor of the Evening News, they take it on trust. Don't shoot it, don't report it – just wrap it up and slap the CBS eye on it. And hope you won't notice the difference.

The key word above is outsourcing. Networks buy footage and scripts from others. Newspapers share bureaus and pool their coverage. New media aggregates material from others.

To business types whose goal is to fill a determined space as cost-effectively as possible, this makes perfect sense. And many people don't notice the difference. Sometimes, this works well, sparing tight budgets. After all, that is why AP was set up in 1848. But AP earned its trust because it answered for the ground truth of its "content."

Under the old rules, each news organization made its own reputation and worked hard to keep it. Anyone caught willfully distorting news, much less inventing it, was fired.

Serious editors screened new hires carefully and watched them during trial periods. As a result, a newspaper's masthead or a broadcaster's logo offered a measure of confidence.

With competitors on the same story, mistakes would be quickly exposed. Serious gaffes followed reporters for the rest of their careers. Experienced foreign correspondents knew one another and valued their standing among peers.

These days, news organizations adopt practices common in other industries. Airlines boast about their individual brands yet routinely merge flights with others: code share. When Air France sends passengers on Delta, its brand loses real meaning. But the result is only a different sort of service. If the product is news, who assures ground truth?

Fenton's book came out in 2005 before the situation got decidedly worse. He joined CBS in the 1960s when it still lived up to its Edward R. Murrow traditions. Like NBC and ABC, its well-staffed bureaus in strategic cities covered news as it took shape. This lasted into the 1990s.

By 2010, CBS had staff correspondents in London and Tokyo, with a few freelancers on call elsewhere. When something major happens, a crew might scramble to report the aftermath. But, Fenton writes, "Stories that seek to explain the relevance of incremental development in far-off countries rarely see the light of day."

If CBS is now seldom there, neither are its competitors. NBC scaled back drastically. Then, in 2010, ABC let go nearly 400 people in the United States and abroad, almost a quarter of its reporting staff. The London bureau, ABC's foreign hub, was stripped to the bone.

×

Being honest, in this context, is expensive. So who pays? The debate rages on. Business models will evolve and then

likely change again. Writers can work for free, whether
for nobility or vanity; an astonishing number of them do.
But most must draw on secondhand sources, guesswork,
or their own imaginations. Free does not cover the plane
ticket or local help to find the right sources, translate,
and persuade drugged teenagers to lower their Kalash-
nikovs at roadblocks.

One answer is a new category that has joined the old ranks:
independent journalists. Some are old-style freelancers
who string for news organizations. But others simply show
up at a story, post their dispatches online, and collect
financial backing from small advertisers and readers who
like their stuff.

This is a heaven-sent opportunity for students and others
anxious to make a career of global reporting. Surprisingly
few people want to face the hardship and risks in places
where news often happens. With a few bucks to get started, eager neophytes can carve out a niche. But eagerness
is just the price of admission. Without a firm grasp on
ethics, responsibility, and ground truth, serious editors
will shun them like malaria-bearing mosquitoes.

New ventures mean fresh possibilities for independent
journalists, whether they are privately owned like GlobalPost
or nonprofits like ProPublica (www.propublica.org). A few
are likely to flourish, and others may fail. New ones will
appear. All have an important point in common: Editors
take chances on entry-level reporters who work cheap
and learn fast.

For the rest of us, news consumers, the best of these
ventures offer something more. They are run by old hands
whose reputations alone provide institutional credibility.

These alternative news outlets will hardly replace the
mainstream anytime soon. GlobalPost's newsgathering
budget in 2010 was one-fiftieth of AP's. Still, limited size
is less limiting than it may seem. A reporter can focus on
a single story. And if it meets the tests for ground truth,

it can faithfully reflect the larger picture. A story, in such instances, can tell the story.

A Story,
The Story

chapter nine

Ryszard Kapuscinski, an icon of Africa reporting, was famed for shunning beaten tracks. He lived in a Lagos slum and poked into places few others went. But working for a low-budget Polish news agency, he also dogged Reuters and AP correspondents whose resources added the breadth he needed. He could focus on *a* story, his own revealing sidelight vignette. But he also had *the* story, news that shed light on major global currents.

This distinction is fundamental to any journalist. On a specific assignment, or pursuing a single subject, you have the luxury to focus tightly and dig deep. As an agency reporter, you squeeze features in with official briefings, routine busywork, and a steady watch of local media. Either way, each type needs to learn the skills of the other.

Office-bound agency grunts periodically get to breathe deeply and soar. Along with their eyes and ears, they can engage their noses and nerve endings. A Kapuscinski who spends most of his time doing this can help them pull back curtains and lift up rugs to reveal facets of societies they thought they knew well.

Slow-motion stylists prefer local guesthouses or travelers' hotels where they are closer to the people they are writing about. They assiduously avoid the pack, finding untapped sources and local friends, living the life they write about. They avoid many reporters' tendency to interview each other.

Mainstream types gravitate toward the same hotel, as fancy as their expense accounts allow. Many seek comfort in the pack. Room service and laundry delivery help a lot when you write until all hours in your room. Most important, there is always a late-night watering hole.

Both types of reporter need to cross paths regularly to stay abreast of things. One cannot overestimate the importance of that hotel bar. At some point, everyone is thrust into the middle of major doings whatever the original quest. There is an old yarn about a reporter sent to cover a bigwig airport arrival. As deadline nears, his editor asks why he doesn't have the story. Oh, the guy says, no story. The plane crashed.

A star exhibit in the correspondents' museum of horrors

dates back to 1961: U.N. Secretary General Dag Hammar-skjold's flight to Ndola, in what is now Zambia, to mediate mayhem in the breakaway Congo province of Katanga.

It was a huge story in a world that was just beginning to notice Africa. Belgium freed the Congo in 1960, and it promptly fell apart. A fiery leader named Patrice Lumumba rattled the West. Belgian interests, anxious to hold onto Katanga's rich copper mines, helped Moise Tshombe secede. His army of gendarmes held off European mercenaries hired by the central government. A U.N. force was deployed to keep them apart.

For much of its news of dramatic events in Katanga, the world relied on the AP stringer, an Englishmen who owned a local laundry. This was the stuff of *Scoop.* But when Hammarskjold announced he would go to Katanga, AP sent Andrew Boroweic, a Geneva-based correspondent who covered Africa. He arrived to find Colin Frost and Dennis Lee Royle, a reporter-photographer team from the London bureau, already there.

That night, journalists from everywhere jammed the airport to await the secretary general. When a plane landed, police kept the press far back from the tarmac and the departing motorcade. A police officer told reporters Hammarskjold had arrived. Frost phoned Boroweic at the cable office. AP filed an urgent story. So did its fierce competitor, United Press International.

Frost followed the motorcade while Boroweic wrote a long colorful story, with details of Katanga fighting and U.N. efforts to stop it. Frost called in an update to say "they" were meeting in the town of Kitwe; he would wait to see what developed. At 2 a.m., Boroweic got back to the hotel. After working at full speed since 5 a.m., he ignored the usual gang at the hotel bar and went straight to his room.

Soon after, Frost woke him for money to pay his taxi. He said everything was on course. At 6:30 a.m., however, Royle pounded on Boroweic's door with the local paper.

Hammarskjold had not landed. An American colonel at the bar told reporters that the dignitary who arrived and traveled in the motorcade was, in fact, a British envoy. Hammarskjold's plane had crashed in remote savannah, and he was dead.

The UPI reporter and others at the bar were able to get word to their desks to kill their arrival stories before anyone published them. AP's remained on the wire.

The AP desk had put Boroweic's name, not Frost's, on the flawed story. Living now in Cyprus, he is still haunted by the memory. He wrote me recently: "Needless to say I was shattered and sent a cable to (AP executive editor) Alan Gould offering to resign, given the avalanche of criticism by world media. His cabled answer was, 'Onkeep shirt, letter follows.'"

Andy's note, harking back half a century, says much about what has changed. With today's communications, a mistake like that can be quickly corrected. But it nonetheless causes irreparable damage. By yesterday's standards, it would not be made in the first place. And if it were, those involved would remember it for the rest of their lives.

Too many journalists, self-styled and otherwise, now pass along unchecked "facts" as soon as they pop up. After all, you can always update. It should not work that way.

Half of AP's watchword was always: Get it first. Today, too many people make a fetish of that while forgetting the second half: But get it right.

Gould's cablese support for a guy willing to fall on his sword says yet more. He knew his correspondents well, and he followed each story. An old pro himself, he understood how news is gathered. Mistakes happen; you admit them, explain them, and do not make them again. Too many bosses these days quickly toss a reporter to the wolves to give an impression of credibility. But Gould knew Boroweic had earned real credibility on the road.

What with satellite phones and email, reporters no longer dread unfolding a cable that reads, WHY YOUR EXCLUSIVE STILL EXCLUSIVE QUERY. The crux of this is an unchanging truth: Even if you are the next incarnation of Ryszard Kapuscinski, check out the hotel bar.

x

Given the choice, I much prefer to work alone. The annals of great reporting are in rich in crafty loners who found unusual ways to bore beneath the surface. When news organizations staff bureaus adequately, that is how it works.

The *Wall Street Journal* sent good people into Saudi Arabia as Coalition forces prepared to invade Kuwait. It had enough reporters to cover briefings and go out on pools. This allowed Tony Horwitz to do the best work of the war. He angled his way to the border, switching from one army to another, and decided the Egyptians were his best shot. He befriended officers who were happy someone bothered to cover them. As Horwitz figured, they would lead the advance into Kuwait. He rode a tank past cheering crowds a day before the rest of us arrived.

My job as AP's special correspondent was designed for this. When big news broke, I was to find a story that told the story. Meantime, my colleagues did the harder job of keeping track of all developments to send a series of leads throughout the day for 10,000 newspapers and broadcast stations that relied on them. But it did not always work that way.

Late in December 1989, I watched TV in the Paris bureau as Nicolae Ceausescu harangued Romanians in Bucharest. He was the last holdout after the Berlin Wall fell and the rest of East Europe was finally free. As the durable dictator spoke, the crowd surged forward. Ceausescu took half a step backward, and the electricity was almost visible. The balance of fear had shifted.

I hurried to the photo desk. The desk editor called photo

agencies to split charter costs while I rounded up two friends: Phil Revzin of the *Wall Street Journal* and Bill Landry of the *St. Petersburg Times.* Both were great report-ers, and neither had a syndicate that might scoop AP.

At 6 a.m. New York time, I woke up Nate Polowetzky, my foreign editor.

"Nate," I said, "It's Mort."

"Gzzuppmph," he replied.

"Say yes," I said.

He paused for half a beat and then, more awake, replied in his scratchy-squeaky voice: "Yes."

No questions. I hung up and committed $5,000 as our share of an aircraft. We convinced French air controllers to clear us without Romanian authorization. Late that night, we landed at Bucharest airport in the dark, with no visas. At the immigration counter, I tried good cheer. "How's it going?" I asked the deadpan border guard. "Better now," he said, and he stamped our passports.

We commandeered a bus to a hotel at the edge of town and then flagged down a little Dacia sedan. The driver spoke English. I asked what was happening, and he said, "Oh, a small revolution in a small place."

We had lucked out. After the early confusion, the airport shut down. Some reporters got in by road. But for days on end coverage was left to a very little bunch of madmen.

The first night's story wrote itself — in two senses. The elements fell into place; I only had to take note of them. Later, I relayed the main points and sidelight detail to Alison Smale in the Vienna bureau, and she waxed poetic under my name.

I found a friendly kid and helped him lug a heavy sports

bag across a main square. It was full of AK-47 assault rifles. He signed on as translator. We got into the state television tower, which was under fire from holdouts of Ceausescu's Securitate. The man who would be president was on the third floor; he briefed our little band. I found a telephone line and dictated to Vienna until shells blew away the room.

Then I found a telex with no paper and continued filing to Vienna, unable to read what I wrote. When gunshots whizzed past, I crouched under the table and kept typing, hands overhead, by touch and guesswork.

The next morning, Bucharest was chaotic. People dashed short distances and ducked into doorways. Upper windows were thick with Securitate snipers. I teamed up with Blaine Harden of the *Washington Post*. Each day, we found a piece of the story to reflect the bigger picture. At the hospital we counted corpses and interviewed survivors. "Democracy," one youth said. "I just want to savor that word in my mouth." The next day, we went to funerals.

We toured Ceausescu's enormous palace and the publishing house where his silly thoughts, in mountains of books, were translated into a dozen languages. One morning, we found the secret room where people believed police had listened to bugged conversations across the country and every phone call. We found six open-reel tape recorders, some broken, and a bank of prehistoric Soviet phones.

On Christmas Day, word reached Bucharest that the fleeing first couple had been captured and shot. It was over. I assembled my notes for a wrap-up story and realized that the first place we had all gone to find a story turned out to be the story. On Dec. 27, I filed this:

BUCHAREST, Romania — The television station that once beamed the glory of Nicolae Ceausescu to a numbed nation has become not only the voice, but the soul of the revolution that toppled his government and ended his life.

While everything it broadcast once was suspect, nothing now is believed until it appears
on Free Romania Television, as the station is
calling itself. Although he was reported captured and executed, it wasn't until television
showed Ceausescu in captivity that the nation
sighed in relief.

The station first broke from the propaganda of
the Stalinist past Friday morning, when army
units joined protesters to drive Ceausescu
from his palace and from power.

"We've won. We've won," poet Murica Dinescu
suddenly shouted into the camera. But those
giddy opening moments only were a prelude to the
battles with Ceausescu loyalists that followed.

The National Salvation Committee clung to the
television like a mantle of power, running the
country from a barricaded studio while Ceausescu's fanatical guard tried to blast it into
silence. Sniper fire smashed windows and heavy
shells blew holes in the walls.

Early Saturday morning, news editor Victor
Ionescu announced on the air: "We are under
attack."

He urged people to rally outside the TV station in a massive human shield to protect the
building. Almost immediately, a crowd formed.

People chanted, "Freedom! Freedom!" until
gunfire broke out. Each time, they scattered
and regrouped. They shouted, "We won't go,"
and they didn't. Outgunned, the attackers
pulled back.

Later that weekend, Ceausescu's guard struck
again. Infiltrators stabbed people in the hall-

ways of the 13-story complex, reportedly killing three. For a few hours, TV screens went
mysteriously blank.

But the interruption was merely a technical
problem, it was explained. Romania was still
governed from a hectic studio littered with
empty bottles, cracked coffee mugs and half-
eaten sandwiches and run by people who had not
slept in days.

Television has played a large role in the
forces of reform that swept the East Bloc this
year. Mass demonstrations were shown live on
TV in Czechoslovakia in the days preceding the
Communist leadership's downfall; East Germans
able to watch West German broadcasts followed
closely news of the loosening of travel restrictions and the rallies that brought down
Erich Honecker; a Solidarity economic minister
goes on the air with regular "fireside chats"
to the people.

Free Romania Television has become a chaotic
reflection of the country it covers, a jumbled
but jubilant mirror of the revolution it
helped orchestrate.

"It is madness here, madness," said Gratiela
Ripeanu. Her external relations job used to
consist mainly of shaking hands with fraternal
Bulgarians.

Suddenly, she was shepherding countless
foreign TV crews all desperate to relay film
back home. Reporters counted on her to find
them National Salvation Committee members to
interview.

One by one, she steered people and their bulky
gear through an obstacle course of gun bar-

rels, locked gates, roiling crowds and skit-
tish guards who looked for explosives in ball-
point pen refills. Six body searches separated
the street from the studio.

"We don't know what we are doing anymore, but
we're doing it," she said.

Elena Maria Ionescu, a news writer and Victor's wife, helped out in the studio, partly
because her office was a gaping hole in the
eighth floor. She smiled broadly when she recognized several reporters who had sat with her
until morning during the first assault.

They had subsequently stayed in the relative
luxury of hotel rooms, but she was still on
the job.

"I've slept here, ate here, washed things out
here," she said. "My husband is so hoarse he
can hardly talk on the air." Nevertheless, she
seemed ready for another four days.

Most of the station's 1,300 employees were
caught up in the mad metamorphosis.

Until the revolution, the station broadcast
only two hours daily, a deadening litany of
the heroic and generous qualities of Ceausescu. Romania's austerity budget left it short
of equipment and supplies.

Suddenly, it was on the air around the clock,
and Romanians who once scorned television sat
glued to their screens.

Technicians cannibalized old gear and pushed
technical tolerances to the limit. Armed soldiers wandered across the set, and overtired
officials reverted to the hated communist term

for comrade, "tovarase," rather than "domnul," or mister, but the show went on.

During the assault, section chiefs and janitors alike beamed with pride at the unflickering image they broadcast across the fearful nation. In the face of rumors and threats, the reassuring voices on television maintained the momentum of the revolt.

Unlikely heroes emerged in the heat of battle. Marin Constantin, who edited youth programs, took it upon himself to make sure the eighth-floor occupants made it through the night.

When the shooting started, he herded everyone into a central hallway protected from ricochets by a double layer of walls. When he found no other way to extinguish the grilled ceiling light, he deftly smashed it with a chair.

When the heavy fighting began, his grin broadened, comforting others whose thoughts were beginning to rattle them. To amuse the company, he sang an old national hymn that was almost forgotten during Ceausescu's reign.

It went, "Wake up, Romania, from the mortal sleep into which you have been lulled by the evil tyrant."

The song, broadcast earlier in the day over the battered transmitters, seemed to fit Free Romania Television.

×

When dramatic news breaks suddenly, a single well chosen facet can reflect the big picture. After those first few days in Romania, journalists by the hundreds swarmed into

Bucharest. But one microdot had set the tone. David Turnley won the 1989 Pulitzer for news photography with a close-up of a weeping man whose face was caught between grief and joy. His brother, Peter, made almost exactly the same picture as they rode together into Bucharest past crowds thronging the road.

(David Turnley later managed to capture Gulf War One with a single image. Because access was so limited, few cameras caught the human distress behind all the wide-angle smoke and fire. Turnley rode a medevac flight and photographed a wounded soldier. He defied the censors and filed it.)

But breaking stories quickly change shape and take on unexpected dimensions.

When I talked with Alison Smale 20 years after that hectic week in Romania, we analyzed in hindsight how AP covered the story. She was kind in attributing to me careful thought in planning an approach. In fact, I operated on instinct, responding to circumstance with a great deal of help.

Few people realize how often bylines atop dramatic dispatches are only tips of icebergs. On the first night, I flung handfuls of wet clay to Vienna, the control bureau for Eastern Europe. Smale and her small staff sculpted it into shape. I could forget about history, international context, and all the rest. I concentrated on a strong intro and what I could see, hear, and smell for myself. And then, as is often the case, communications defined the week's coverage.

The Intercontinental Hotel had two working telex circuits, with hundreds of journalists, businessmen, and stranded travelers clamoring for them. A line snaked around the upstairs lobby for three international telephones. A few correspondents unscrewed the mouthpieces to attach alligator clips so they could transmit by prehistoric Tandy computers. Mostly, reporters dictated their stories, as competitors on deadline banged on phone-booth doors.

I headed out at 6 each morning so I could file by lunchtime when I still had a fair shot at a telex. (With today's communications, it is usually much easier to file. But don't count on it.) After that first crazed week, all of us were able to breathe deeply and write the larger story. Ceausescu's Romania was all smoke, mirrors, and the Wizard of Oz.

×

Different societies have their own approach to reporting. Each has something to teach us. With the Internet, we can read those long detailed German dispatches written for people who care about process and do not bore easily. *Die Zeit,* a weekly newspaper, like *Der Spiegel,* a newsmagazine, probes hard at things that matter. That is Germany's general style, as it is for serious media in Switzerland, Sweden, Norway, and Finland.

British style is rooted in first person reporting, which is a mixed blessing. The classic reductio ad absurdum is that short message cabled by a correspondent to establish his byline: "I arrived in this war-torn capital today. Pick up agencies." That is, write the story from Reuters and AP dispatches.

Still, this style can be effective, helpful to understanding the backdrop. Many in America are especially fond of Robert Fisk of the *Independent,* who works hard to see things for himself. His dispatches, very much Fisk, are best read within in a wider context. Others, such as Jon Swain of the London *Sunday Times,* get close yet keep a cool distance from points of view.

French reporters refer to "*un sujet,*" a story. Some simply pick a subject for what amounts to an essay that earns space under their name. Others choose pieces that fit together onto a broader canvas for readers they expect to stay with them as events take shape.

In short, good reporters should be on the offensive, always out there snuffling after the scent the way a pig looks for truffles. That is how you learn whether a fear-some tyrant actually has weapons of mass destruction or whether a superpower's purported ally is secretly fortifying the common enemy. You notice large phenomena such as climate change while there is still time to act, and you keep after the story until people take notice.

In covering famine over three decades, I have yet to see one that was inevitable – or that did not leave lasting scars among the improbable survivors who'd been left to die. All famine can be foreseen; if food reaches threatened populations before they must go in search of it, calamity need not happen.

But today we are on the defensive. Editors expend scant budgets only on stories when they break. That is, when it is too late to do anything more than watch them get worse.

In this vacuum, editors take what they get for free, packaged handouts from authorities or non-governmental organizations. This results in skewed priorities. Reporters who gather news personally learn fast to look critically at such largesse. Often, the most effective aid comes from people too busy to boast about it. Some charities focus more on fundraising than helping victims. After brutal famine eased in Somalia during the 1980s, one group kept tugging at heartstrings. Its camera crew spent six weeks finding a cow skinny enough to spark donors' sympathy. By then, help was badly needed elsewhere.

The larger lesson here is clear. It is easy enough to get a story. The story is something else entirely.

x

For a clear illustration, look at a piece by Anthony Shadid that *The New York Times* ran in 2010, quite literally about a cultural bridge. It looks at a tiny bit of Baghdad yet it sheds light on much of the Middle East. Shadid won two Pulitzers for international reporting, both in Iraq for the

Washington Post. He was already at the *Times* when the second was announced.

BAGHDAD — On a bend in the Tigris where caliphs summered when Baghdad was the City of Peace, the pontoons came first. Steel and asphalt followed. Now, two years on, the Greihat Bridge, a gesture of wartime expediency, has become permanent, traversing the river, joining two Shiite Muslim neighborhoods and, some fear, going too far.

The footbridge's rationale is mundane: to carry Shiites from Greihat to the sacred, gold-leafed shrine in Kadhimiya, bypassing routes through Sunni neighborhoods. Its symbolism is momentous, though. Traffic is already channeled around sectarian fault lines. Blast walls besiege every neighborhood. But the Greihat Bridge, just 15 feet across and 575 feet long, is possibly the first piece of infrastructure built to reflect and accommodate the reality of a divided Baghdad, suggesting the permanence of what has been wrought. "It's a symbol of war," said Mohammed Kasim, a photographer and filmmaker.

Winston Churchill once remarked that "we shape our buildings and afterward our buildings shape us." The same could be said for the Greihat Bridge, which tells a story of Baghdad's present and its past, a city defined by the vagaries of power, where bridges — named for revolutions and martyrs, architecture and faith — are signposts of rulers' authority.

"We design our city and the city designs us," Muwafaq al-Taei, an architect, said, nodding, offering his own version of Churchill's words. He went on, conflating centuries and rulers. "The story of Baghdad is always a political

story, a completely political story." He
paused again before refining his idea further.

"The story of Baghdad," he said finally, settling on his thought, "is the story of infrastructure."

The city's bridges recall past triumphs and tragedies,
Shadid explained. The Two-Story Bridge evokes Saddam
Hussein. The Martyrs Bridge is where police shot up a
Communist Party protest in 1948, led by a woman remembered as "a virtuous prostitute." But none, he wrote, has
more meaning than the Greihat, the 13th and last across
the Tigris. It was planned by the nationalist who deposed
the monarchy in 1958, part of a grand vision to modernize
Baghdad. But the Baath Party overthrew him in 1963 and
was not eager to link Shiites across the river.

"Those who control power always try to control
the city through demographic changes," said
Saad Eskander, the director of the National
Library and Archive.

"Soon the Shias will control the city," he
added. "In fact, they already do."

In that, Baghdad is unlike any other Arab capital. Black, green and red flags of Shiite piety
flutter under solar-powered streetlights, which
cast a pallid glow on slogans for Imam Hussein,
Shiite Islam's most revered figure. A square named
after Saladin, the Sunni hero of the Crusades,
was renamed after Malik al-Ashtar, a loyal
companion of Ali, Imam Hussein's father, whom
Shiites consider the successor to the Prophet
Muhammad. The Two-Story Bridge, that icon of
the former president, is now a preserve of a
group loyal to Ammar al-Hakim, a Shiite leader. The Martyrs Bridge carries traffic through
an arcade of columns plastered with portraits
of Moktada al-Sadr, a radical Shiite cleric.

And, in the upheaval unleashed by the United States invasion, Greihat was built, joining two Shiite locales by circumventing the staunchly Sunni neighborhood of Adhamiya.

"The problems started between the people, and that meant there was fear," said Jassem Ali, carrying his 6-year-old son, Hassan, as he crossed the bridge. Religious lamentations drifted across the river, eddying lazily in a soft winter sun, along banks where so many corpses once washed up that residents refused to eat fish from the Tigris.

"To go to Adhamiya meant you had to consider dying," Mr. Ali said. "There was so much killing there."

Construction started in 2008, and restaurants like the Tigris Beach were built at the bridgehead. It is to be expanded so cars can cross to Kadhimiya and its shrines. Meantime, pedestrians stream across with a new sense of security.

"The events,' " Azhar Mohammed said, using a euphemism for the war, "are still here until now. No one's forgotten. A lot of people still have pain in their hearts."

She passed pilgrims carrying carpets and cooking oil, a man in a wheelchair and a woman who went by Um Ali, corralling her three children.

"We can't go to Adhamiya anymore," she said, "but we can still cross the bridge."

Case
Study
One

After
Rwanda:
Under
the
Volcano

PAGE 124

"No one who covered those days in Goma will ever forget the smell of that banana patch," I wrote in AP's staff newsletter back in 1994. "When cholera began its awful scythe sweep among the million Rwandans huddled in squalid camps on volcanic rock, the sight was too overwhelming to register. Sensory overload mercifully converted rows upon rows of corpses into something else, inanimate elements of a story to be written. There wasn't much sound. Most people were too weak even to moan. But nothing blunted the smell, a blood-chilling, hair-bristling, stomach-seizing, toe-curling, putrid and acrid stench of thousands of bodies left to rot in the sun."

For a reporter, this posed a problem. I had seen a lot of world-class cataclysm, but this defied all description. Adjectives like calamity or catastrophe had been devalued with overuse. Superlatives were pointless. Was this hell? That was one dateline I had yet to encounter.

Most such stories have good guys and bad guys. But these pathetic, desperate refugees were Hutus. Many of them had played an enthusiastic role in a burst of genocide that killed 800,000 Tutsis, countrymen of a different tribe. And yet others among the 1.2 million who fled were innocents caught up in events that the outside world failed to stop.

Numbers and statistics had little meaning. U.N. officials could only make wild guesses. Communications were spotty and transportation scarce. We suffered "Goma lungs" from breathing black lava dust mixed with cookfire smoke and dried excrement. We camped in sleeping bags, bathed in mosquito repellent, and drank water brought from Nairobi, two countries away.

The hardest part was staying dispassionate yet human at the same time. "In Goma," I concluded, "there was no good place to stand. It was a human cataclysm that did not have to happen and, for all the good will, a lot of people who meant to help were doing the wrong thing."

Rather than write what was happening, my AP colleagues and I tried to show it. Close-up reportage would tell the story by reflection. If readers could feel the trauma of a few people sketched in detail, they might be able to better comprehend those panoramic camera sweeps.

One story began: "Like everywhere else, the Boy Scouts of Zaire are prepared, ready to help wherever they can. Here their good deed is to collect bodies by the thousand and dump them into a pit ...'It is only normal, isn't it?' asked Jean Wauters, a retired Belgian importer in a roller kerchief who supervised 500 young volunteers. 'Scouts do their part.'"

I profiled Ray Wilkinson, the U.N. refugee agency spokesman. Aid workers are normally only incidental to larger story. But Wilkinson had seen a great deal of war and calamity as a senior *Newsweek* correspondent. I found him shaken and pale one evening, and he told me why. "Ray Wilkinson's bad days are worse than most people's," my dispatch began, "and Thursday was his worst." One horror followed another until the climax: a body truck hurtled toward his jeep at 40 miles an hour, missing it by inches. It slammed into a ditch, and bloated corpses catapulted against his windshield and onto the roof. Aid workers riding with him screamed in terror.

Later, I drove for hours up the road to Katale where U.S. Air Force C-130s were to deliver relief supplies from their base in Germany. U.N. teams and volunteers had organized effective aid delivery across the whole area. They asked that the planes land at Goma where crews could unload them and stockpile the cargo. Instead, the Americans chose a remote dirt strip.

The Air Force gave no arrival time for security reasons; trucks were immobilized to wait. When the giant transports arrived, pilots decided to dump the cargo without landing. Ten tons — only half of the load — were pushed out of cargo doors. All but five tons were lost in the bush. One heavy crate almost hit a school and another barely missed a U.N. helicopter.

My story began: "A U.S. airdrop criticized beforehand as a publicity stunt missed the target by a half-mile Sunday, scattering bundles over terrified Rwandan refugees who thought they were being bombed. 'I can't believe it,'

British aid worker John Wallis said, as he slashed at wrappings with a bowie knife, and flour spilled into a muddy cornfield. 'This is criminal. I'm speechless.'"

Before leaving Goma, I sat down to sketch an overview. Contemplating the cone rising majestically above the lush Eastern Congo forest, I chose the slug-line Under the Volcano, evoking Malcolm Lowry's novel about Mexico:

GOMA, Zaire - At first glance, it is just a busy market day in this backwater crossroads, with all of the routine haggling, honking and thievery that fades into late-night laughter.

The Two Seasons Restaurant is chockablock with truckers wolfing down spicy beans and rice, a whitewashed hole in the wall by the packed stalls of women selling bananas, chilis and bright cloth.

Goma's golden youth hang out at the hotels, emptying quart-size bottles of Primus in beery oblivion. Around midnight, the Feeling Club jams to overflow in ear-splitting, gyrating revelry.

All is normal under the volcano, in a breathtaking setting on Lake Kivu, a few steps from the heart of darkness, not far from where Stanley met Livingstone and gorillas romp in the mist.

Then you notice that the bundles by the road aren't blankets. People who seem to be napping in the sun will not wake up. The smell that seeps into every cranny, putrid and acrid, is death en masse.

On any road out of town, there is no missing the cataclysm. No one knows whether the sudden tide of Rwandans that washed over Goma is the

worst humanitarian calamity ever. A million
have come, and thousands are dying. But numbers alone mean nothing.

The problem is not a lack of food, despite all
the publicity over a botched U.S. airdrop that
ended up adding only five tons of stocks to a
camp that is well-supplied by road.

Cholera, the doctors say, is just a fancy word
for virulent dysentery caused by people drinking the only water they can find after their
desperate flight - feces-laced, mud-colored goo.

As bad as the camp is, only a few are leaving.
Mostly, in the end, Rwandan refugees are dying
from fear.

Despite the assurances by outsiders who have
come to help, the people of Goma do not expect
this Biblical exodus to reverse itself anytime
soon. Ethnic cleansing over the border is
nothing new.

Valentin Lubao, in a white shirt and impor-
tant-person's suit, supervises the outdoor
market in the heart of town, a focal point for
Rwandans seeking a handout or a piece of tin
roof for shelter.

The strain on this city of 180,000 has driven
up the price of food staples threefold in a
few weeks.

"They must go back," he told a visitor, while
admitting that most probably would not leave
for at least six months. "We are catching their
diseases. Their bodies litter our streets."

As the visitor left, Lubao had questions of
his own: "Why did Clinton, the others, all

wait so long? Couldn't they see what was happening? Didn't they care?"

In squalid, cheek-by-jowl camps outside of town, refugees are settling in to stay. Water tanks are appearing. Plastic sheets and sticks turn into huts. But the lava rock is too hard for latrines.

On most days, the refugees have taken away the volcano. Smoke from cookfires blots out the view of Nyiragongo, a perfect cone looming high above luxuriant vegetation.

Fuel is whacked by machete from the nearest trunk, leaving ugly stumps and fatally wounded trees over vast roadside stretches. Goma's shade and natural décor are going fast.

At the circular park in the center of town, early one morning, one young man stretched, stepped over a body in the dust and walked over to urinate on the last living oleander.

Everywhere, the contrasts are startling.

Outside the Hotel du Grands Lacs, a corpse lay untouched for days. Inside, 250 wedding guests in Sunday finery whooped it up in raucous opulence.

Along the lakeside Corniche, color-coordinated bougainvillea spills over the walls of elegant houses left from colonial days. On the banks, refugees cover every inch of ground, and they jostle to draw water with bodies floating nearby.

On a clear day at Katale, up north, you can lift your eyes from squalor and see hibiscus and birds of paradise. Far beyond, Nyiragongo epitomizes the soaring beauty of Central Africa.

At the Hotel Nyira in Goma, Mitzi Koutses had to trim her menu because of the crisis. But "extra-soft smoked salmon," osso bucco, chocolate mousse and her best Bordeaux wines survived the cut.

She apologizes to customers for the slow service.

"Everyday a waiter comes in with a sore back, a headache, and cannot work," she explained. "It is all psychological. These bodies, all the people everywhere, it is making them crazy."

On Goma's crowded streets, people wear scarves over their faces, like Old West bandits, or surgical masks to filter the deadly dust and blunt the stench.

Refugees and townsfolk alike carry five-gallon yellow plastic jerricans to collect water whenever the taps happen to run.

Aid workers say many lives could have been saved had wealthy governments acted more quickly to provide water and health care. But this is Zaire, they add, where nothing is easy.

When one relief flight arrived last week, a visiting Zairian colonel demanded a payment of $17,000 to let it leave. After haggling, he settled for $400. Later, his own plane would not start, and he asked for help. The price was $400.

Although cameras focus on the desperate, refugees include young intellectuals, soldiers carrying looted booty, wheeler-dealer businessmen and ex-Cabinet ministers with full pockets.

At the Feeling Club, "Cousin" the D.J. laughed when asked if the refugee influx had dampened business. "Who do you think is spending all this money?" he replied.

These higher-profile refugees will likely be the last to return. Instead, the deposed elite may dig in just over the border and plot the next act in a long-running drama.

For centuries, Tutsis and Hutus have cohabited lush land in the shadow of dramatic mountain peaks. Tutsis, tall and skilled at war, were masters. Hutus, though far more numerous, were their vassals.

The balance shifted in 1962 when Hutus took power in a new state, freshly independent from the Belgians who had governed through the Tutsis. Periodic massacres followed.

In 1991, a band of Tutsi rebels began to advance. President Juvenal Habyarimana negotiated and allowed a unit of armed Tutsis to camp in Kigali, the capital. Hutu extremists stirred the waters.

Suddenly, Habyarimana and the president of neighboring Burundi died in a mysterious plane crash. Hutu death squads let loose with machetes and soon maybe half a million Tutsis were dead.

The world denounced genocide but sent no troops to stop it. Instead, the Tutsi rebels knifed toward Kigali and took over the country. Hutus fled for the borders.

Now more than three million Hutus are refugees, nearly half the pre-drama population. They went to Tanzania, Uganda and Burundi, but about half are around Goma, under the volcano.

As a backdrop to the calamity, the volcano Nyiragongo seems to be belching and bubbling more than usual, adding an element of tension to a situation that does not need it. At night, it glows ominously.

"Someone described the scene around here as hell without fire," observed Ron Redmond of the U.N. High Commissioner for Refugees office. "If the volcano blows, they will have that, too."

Airtime

chapter ten

Television news, done right, is the most powerful medium we have. Cameras can take us, step by step, into territory we cannot conjure from words or photos alone. Radio might capture voices and sounds, the urgency of the street. But TV shows us the street. We watch people tell their own stories, terrified or triumphant. A well-edited piece, given the time it needs, teleports us to the story's midst. A knowledgeable narrator can tell us how to fit those small pictures into a larger frame.

When tremors leveled much of Haiti's capital in 2010, the world responded massively and immediately. That was because of television done right. More and more, however, TV news is not done right. Or it is not done at all.

Television coverage is expensive to do well, and it takes more than money. It may seem easy as those seamless images flicker across the screen, but it isn't.

Margaret Moth of CNN died in 2010, after eluding so many close calls as a fearless camerawoman. She took a bullet to the face in Sarajevo and, with intricate reconstructive surgery, she returned to Bosnia. At 59, cancer finally got her. Cynde Strand, her old friend, wrote this tribute:

Each of us wanted to be one of the boys. We all wanted to be cameramen, because in the early 80s there were hardly any camerawomen covering international news. CNN, the then-unknown TV maverick, gave us a chance. We paid our dues and we worked hard. We kept turning up on all the big stories, on the front lines, in the midst of disasters and revolutions, in the right place for the best shot. The cameramen made room for us, gave us the nod, and became part of a club that is more like a family.

At one point there were five camerawomen based internationally shooting for CNN ... We worked with the best reporters on the biggest stories. We were pretty and fun and brave, and we came back with the goods. We were hardcore when it came to camerawork. We pushed the envelope, and we took shots that would take your breath away.

We were all fiercely independent, much too independent to be united as a women's group. What united us was our passion for each picture, each story, our insatiable curiosity about new places, and as journalists, the feeling that we just had to be there.

What did we learn? We learned that life is short and precious, we learned to be as respectful to the street sweeper as to the king or president, we learned that for all the intolerable cruelty that mankind is responsible for, there are also moments of incredible humanity and grace. And we learned that one powerful image can make a difference.

Will we mourn Margaret Moth differently? Yes, in a few ways . . . But we are also smiling as we think about birthdays in Somalia, sunrises in Iraq, mountain peaks in Tibet, floating down the Congo River and rollerblading down the Champs-Élysées. Our smiles celebrate the extraordinariness of our lives and the residue we carry, of at times sharing through the camera lens some of the most intimate moments in people's lives.

Jane, Mary, Maria, Cynde and dear Margaret – we broke news, we broke stereotypes, we broke hearts, and tonight I will drink to one of the girls."

×

By then, Cynde Strand had moved to Atlanta to direct CNN's coverage of international news. She struggles to keep the old spirit alive. These days, that is as challenging as anything she faced on the road.

Television is still the most popular medium, but broadcast news now rarely comes from those knowledgeable narrators. Crews of either gender are growing scarce. It is far cheaper to quote newspapers, subscribe to agencies, and buy generic video feeds from others. As budgets shrink, focus shifts steadily farther away from substance.

The picture varies across the world. The BBC, for one, remains relatively strong, supported by public license fees and shielded from excessive official meddling. Yet even the BBC faces serious cutbacks. Other European networks, along with some from the Middle East, Asia, and Latin America supply wide coverage. In America, viewers' attention spans seem to recede as quickly as advertising income, and a downward spiral continues.

By 2010, U.S. broadcast networks were pathetically thin on the ground, each with a tiny handful of staff reporters to cover a large globe. Many crucial stories are simply ignored. Others are narrated at long distance by correspondents who have never set foot in the places they describe. By twisted TV logic, if they are in London or Tokyo that counts as foreign, even if the story they "cover" might be thousands of miles away.

U.S. cable news networks spend heavily to persuade viewers that they provide what the big three do not. Yet a close examination shows serious gaps in their coverage, sporadic at best, with heavy emphasis on one big story at a time and filler features in between.

The Pew Research Center's Project for Excellence in Journalism (www.journalism.org) keeps tabs on who covers what, for broadcast news as well as for print media. The International Reporting Project at Johns Hopkins University (www.irp.org) tracks trends. Other such organizations, along with some energetic individuals, are listed in the Appendix. But a ballpark measure is easy enough: simply flip through the channels.

On most mornings, you can start watching at sunrise and keep at it until your second coffee break without hearing the name of a foreign country. When a major story imposes, such as a Haitian earthquake or a surge assault in Afghanistan, the focus is on Americans' role in the story. You can find real news on European, Asian, and Middle Eastern networks but only if you look for it online.

Network viewers face a bleak present and a bleaker future unless a critical mass of public outcry can persuade television executives that global news matters. If that seems unlikely, the history of broadcast news suggests it is at least possible.

×

Back in 1961, Newton Minow spoke to the National Association of Broadcasters in Washington. Minow, the controversial head of the Federal Communications Commission, was a political operative turned civil servant with little taste for fluff or violence on TV. His words still echo within the industry:

"When television is good, nothing — not the theater, not the magazines or newspapers — nothing is better. But when television is bad, nothing is worse. I invite each of you to sit down in front of your television set when your station goes on the air and stay there, for a day, without a book, without a newspaper ... I can assure you that what you will observe is a vast wasteland."

A year earlier, Edward R. Murrow had abandoned television, disgusted by CBS constraints. He had made his own memorable speech to TV executives in 1958: "During the daily peak viewing periods, television in the main insulates us from the realities of the world in which we live. If this state of affairs continues, we may alter an advertising slogan to read: Look now, pay later."

Fred Friendly, Murrow's longtime producer, fought for better coverage as president of CBS News until 1966. When the network aired I Love Lucy reruns instead of hearings on the Vietnam War, he stormed out the door.

But a continuing buildup in Vietnam energized television coverage. Networks sent large crews to cover what The New Yorker media critic, Michael Arlen, dubbed "the living room war." Into the 1990s, all three networks had substantial bureaus across the globe. Correspondents rushed to cover big news when it broke. In quiet periods, they dug for stories simmering below the surface. Cameras showed slices of life abroad to give Americans a sense of others who shared their planet.

In the years since 9/11, Minow's diatribe has come back to haunt. We can only guess what he would have thought about American Idol and violent cop shows. But we can be pretty certain about his opinion of news coverage.

Television news can still rivet us to our chairs as no other medium can. Beyond the odd scoop, everyday sidelights still illuminate. Early in 2010, for instance, the U.S. command finally gave up on a remote firebase in Afghanistan after losing 42 men over three years. Richard Engel of NBC interviewed the last men to leave. Their eyes alone told us all we needed to know about lights at the end of tunnels.

Yet, increasingly, we hear echoes of Howard Beale, the anchorman in *Network* who shouted at the camera: "I'm mad as hell, and I'm not going to take it anymore." TV, he railed, is a goddamned amusement. "It is a circus, a carnival, a traveling troupe of acrobats, storytellers, dancers, singers, jugglers, sideshow freaks, lion tamers, and football players. We're in the boredom-killing business."

×

In mid-2009, the Council on Foreign Relations invited former Edward R. Murrow fellows to New York for a two-day program with members. In one panel, the presidents for news of ABC, CBS, and NBC talked about their world coverage. It was an extraordinary example of Orwellian message spinning.

Ken Auletta, the moderator, began with figures from the Pew Center Project for Excellence in Journalism. In 2007,

NBC's Nightly News devoted only 19.8 percent of its coverage to international news, and that slipped to 13.7 percent during 2009. In that same period, CNN dropped by nearly half, from 26.2 percent to 14.8 percent.

"I think you can look at statistics and you come up with it any number of different ways," Sean McManus of CBS replied. "You know, I tend to look at the quality of the journalism." Besides, he said, Washington news should be considered as international. And in the end, he added, you can cram only so much into a 22-minute evening newscast.

Auletta noted that Americans cared more about news close to home and networks responded to that. Then he asked, "Do you feel any obligation as news presidents to, at some time, say to your viewers, eat your spinach and watch this story?" The answers were: "Yeah," "Of course," and "Absolutely, every day." But only one example was cited: Barack Obama was given airtime to explain his domestic health-care plan.

McManus was president of CBS Sports until 2005 when, to some public stir, he also took over CBS News. After detailing how networks had slashed overseas staffs to rely on freelancers, Auletta asked him, "Could you tell us why this works and why it's not a diminishment of foreign reporting?"

"Well, I think it works because there is a different way to gather news now, which you mentioned," McManus said. "You know, we also have to take a step back and realize that, whether we like it or not, we are part of corporations, and we do have some financial responsibility to our corporations."

With technology, he added, large crews are no longer necessary. "And some of the kids that are now coming out of college, who like to be referred to as 'video journalists,' I mean, really are qualified to go into a situation, like the riots in Iran a few months ago, and report some of the best background that you can ever see on television."

And so it went for more than an hour, half-truths and dodge ball from the three men on whom Americans depend most to keep them up to speed on a perilous world.

Kids coming out of college are essential to the process, a new generation that must reshape old media into something we cannot begin to predict. But inexperienced journalists pointing cameras at millennia-old complexity does not replace solid reporting. That is certainly cheaper. But it is dangerous beyond description.

McManus got a laugh when he mentioned the CBS Paris bureau, adding a slight sneer. He said 16 or 17 journalists sat around when they could have been elsewhere. True, Paris is a pleasant base. That bureau off the Champs-Élysées kept some decent wine on hand for distinguished visitors. But it included only a few correspondents, who were often under fire or slogging in mud halfway across the world. Others were seasoned producers and researchers who kept tabs not only on France but also Europe and the world beyond.

Paris is a vital crossroads, a favorite spot for conferences that determine global security, financial stability, and development aid. Like them or not, the French have been major players in world affairs for five centuries. Their armed forces are active in the Middle East, South Asia, and Africa. And France is a major force within the European Union.

Robert Albertson, CBS Paris bureau manager since 1969, emptied out the Rue Marbeuf offices a while back. He was supposed to work from home, but CBS recalled him to New York. That left only a freelance radio correspondent.

CBS president Les Moonves earned $42.9 million in 2009, according to Standard & Poor, second only to Carol Bartz of Yahoo as the highest-paid CEO. Katie Couric's salary of $5 million was equal to the combined budgets of NPR's 17 foreign bureau — and Morning Edition.

×

Vanishing depth on the ground is one main problem. Another is an increasingly skewed focus on celebrity and physical appearance.

In the afterglow of a tribute to Walter Cronkite that filled Lincoln Center, Brian Williams of NBC noted a grim truth in a talk to Arizona students. Today, a gray-haired, mild-mannered grandfather would go largely unnoticed in America, hardly anchor material. Americans like fresh-faced good looks with a touch of safe-sex glamour. The BBC favors "newsreaders" with hard experience stamped on faces that command respect and credibility. But it, too, is under pressure to find new blood and jazz up its sets.

Being attractive is certainly no obstacle to being an excellent journalist. But with appearance weighing so heavily in the equation, coverage often suffers. CNN, for instance, saw Anderson Cooper's ratings soar when he cried on camera, and then asked hard questions during Hurricane Katrina. Suddenly, he was everywhere. CNN promoted him as an expert in the complex science of climate change and sent him around the world. Then he appeared on Times Square to cover the dropping ball at New Year's Eve. No one, however competent, can be everywhere.

Lara Logan worked at CNN but was sidetracked by what insiders say was internal politics tinged with jealousies. It happens. Skilled and courageous, she kept at it as a free-lancer. CBS noticed her and, thrilled by audience response, pushed her to fame. At 35, with experience only in Africa and the Middle East, she was named Chief Foreign Affairs Correspondent. When tabloids revealed a steamy foreign affair with a married U.S. contractor in Baghdad, her private life overshadowed her incisive reporting.

It is a simple fact. Good looks and hot gossip can improve your chances of getting on camera. They may also prove to be a drawback. The important measure is how skilled you are. Aspiring TV journalists might consider this: Approach the job as if you will be wearing a bag over your head. What counts is what you say.

x

Much has been said about television's woes. Ex-practitioners, no longer subject to a boss's reprisal, are particularly articulate on the subject. After four decades of reporting from abroad for CBS, and after his wise analysis, *Bad News*, Tom Fenton followed up in 2009 with a slim volume, *Junk News*. His main worry is that tight budgets mean news is left uncovered until it erupts into plain sight. And, by then, it is too late for public reaction to influence official policy.

Well before 2001, Fenton knocked repeatedly on doors and worked old contacts to arrange an interview with Osama bin Laden. By then, the al Qaeda mastermind had bombed his way to top of every intelligence agencies' A-list. The world needed to know what it was up against. But CBS declined to pay for a crew to fly to Afghanistan.

This is especially tragic when you look at the other side of the coin. Periodically, a story captures viewer interest, and networks pile on, each competing to outdo the other. Money flows in torrents until interest wanes. Then the rest of the world, barring a hotspot or two, is ignored until the next budget infusion.

Television pulled out all stops for the Haiti earthquake, prompting a fast donor response. Within days, however, the real story was a sideshow to the media circus that overshadowed it. CNN boasted it had 12 correspondents and the focus was largely on them. At one point, a screen crawl read: "Breaking News: Dr. Sanjay Gupta helps 14-day-old baby."

Meantime, the BBC and Al Jazeera focused on a fundamental problem of the rescue effort: U.S. troops at the beleaguered Port-au-Prince airport diverted desperately needed aid as they arranged their own logistics.

Haiti needed serious and sustained coverage, with a hard
look at what needed to be done as it dugs itself out after
repeated calamities. This was finally a chance to fortify
infrastructure, with long-term development that might
break its chain of bad governments. Yet soon interest
waned, and TV budgets ran out. Haiti dropped back off the
broadcast map.

×

Since its beginnings, broadcast news has always frustrated
professionals who try to use its full potential. Martin Bell
of the BBC wrote a hard-edged memoir during the Bosnian
war: *In Harm's Way*. An ex-soldier, he has broadcast insight-
ful reportage since Vietnam. Bell's self-mocking subtitle
was Reflections of a War Thug. As he still does today, he
stepped back to look at TV coverage in general.

Bell describes how the process forced him to miss the crucial end to a story he had followed from the beginning:

"Lesson number one was to stay with it. The
reason why I was not a witness to the ambush
was that it happened in the evening, and I had
been compelled to break out to our base in
Ilidza and file for the Six O'Clock News. There
are many arguments for a rolling and continu-
ous news service, but quality of reporting is
not one of them. More means worse. The multi-
plication of deadlines takes us away from the
real world, and drives us back into our offices
and edit rooms. It is safer there, and we may
find reasons to stay. There were days in Sarajevo when my radio colleague, who was already
working for a rolling news service, had to
broadcast as many as twenty-eight separate
reports. Not only did he never leave the Holiday Inn, he hardly had time to pick up the
phone and talk to the U.N. spokesman."

And this was before round-the-clock Internet feeds,

blogs, and Twitter.

Another problem is television's fear of offending viewers. At one point, Paul Goodall, a heroic aid-relief driver, was executed by four volunteer mujaheddin who came from the Middle East to help Bosnian Muslims but took no orders from them. Their brutality was the key to the story. With footage of the aftermath, Bell called London to schedule his story and heard the anxious voice of a duty editor. He tells it like this:

"You are not including any" – there was a hush in the tone and a long awkward pause – "bodies, are you?"

"No," I said. "There's only one. It's in the camp, and the subject of an autopsy. Absolutely no bodies, I assure you."

"Nothing that will upset people?"

"Well, the story itself is pretty upsetting, especially to the families, and they've been told. It is a murder, you know, and a particularly brutal one."

And then the voice said, "Is there blood? We don't want to see any blood, at least not before the nine p.m. watershed. It's in the guidelines, you know."

To be fair, Bell says, the nervousness was based on audience research. At least the BBC did not require script approval as the American networks do. But, he concludes:

In the new climate of sensitivity the BBC could hardly stage the last Act of Hamlet – still less report the death of Paul Goodall in any recognizable way.

I believe we should listen to the audience and

respond to its concerns, but in the internal
BBC debate about the depiction of real world
violence only one side has been heard, and it
hasn't been the side of BBC's troops in the
trenches. The point we would make is that the
new world order is much more dangerous than
the old one, that it has to be seen as it is
rather than as we would wish it to be, and
that in our anxiety not to upset people we are
running the risk of misleading them quite
dangerously.

Fifteen years later, Bell's words resonate steadily louder.
A reporter's job is to report, and each medium should
deploy its comparative strengths. Some images may be too
shocking to relay. But the bar is far too low. War is hell,
whether or not we like it. So is slow death by prevent-
able disease and hunger. Reporters and their editors have
a responsibly to depict things as they are so that people
understand the effect of action, or inaction. Those
that sanitize reality are – no other word applies – lying.

This applies to all media, of course. But the most cautious
is TV, the one with the most potential impact.

×

During those heydays of the late 1960s, television correspondents joined the pack on the road. We all hunted
together. TV reporters traveled with a cameraman and a
sound engineer, at most. They shipped off film in mesh bags
and came down for dinner. Since we covered regions where
we based, most of us knew each other. Kindnesses were
returned; back stabbings were seldom forgotten.

By 1990, this got more complex. A single TV crew could
number above 50 on big stories when you added accoun-
tants with kangaroo belt packs stuffed with money and
gofers who ordered the souvenir T-shirts. Women were
no longer scarce, adding the social drama of mating rituals.
Cliques and clans supplanted camaraderie. Everyone

competed for workspace, drivers, fixers, and access to key sources.

As the first Gulf War took shape in 1991, AP found a huge first-floor suite at the International Hotel in Dhahran, steps away from the Press Center. Dan Rather swept in and told the manager CBS would be quite happy there. How much? The manager had a good laugh, and AP stayed.

Today, the old pack is a crazed free-for-all multinational mob. Freelancers and stringers with Flip cameras jostle for front-rank space at news conferences with television crews that seem to have been hired for sheer size.

Practical field advice is of limited use in such quickly evolving circumstances. Technology changes by the month. Once producers were obsessed with image quality, and elaborate bureaus included people to dab powder puffs on studio guests. Heavy convoys lugged enough satellite gear to direct a moon shot. Today, networks use jerky images that evoke strobe-lit discos but cost practically nothing.

The basics matter more. For these I went to TV people I have learned to admire over the years.

Cindy Babski, who was Lara Logan's producer on *60 Minutes*, worked in print early on as many good broadcast people do. I met her in 1991 when Soviet Georgians were working up to revolution. Crowds protested against the republic's dictator-president, Zviad Gamsakhurdia. He deployed troops to impose calm. Babski was talking with a key figure in the hotel lobby, and I horned in. She smiled sweetly and, with a subtle gesture, suggested that I butt out. Chastened, I helped her with my own sources.

That little interplay was part of the ritual Waugh spoofed to hilarious extreme. Reporters compete for scoops but also cooperate on the routine. Someone you help in a place you know will reciprocate later in one you don't. In Waugh's day, the hard part was finding a way to file; competition outweighed cooperation. It is different now.

When I asked Babski what she would tell young people, I expected to hear about camera angles and booking studio time. Her answer was to study history, political science, languages, and above all, to learn to write well. That is, be a journalist. TV is only a medium.

"Television tends to send people after the fact," she said, "and it is always in the process of catching up. Try to get there before the story happens. If you can't, at least be able to understand the context and know what you're reporting. The danger is not only getting it wrong but also having a negative impact with a commentary that distorts the story."

Budget cuts undermine the fundamentals, Babski says. "It's awful," she said. "There is no sugarcoating it." She recalled the uproar years ago when Cokie Roberts did a Washington story from New York with the Capitol on the screen behind her. Now much worse happens as a matter of routine. Often, correspondents who never leave the London bureau read scripts to "report" stories 10,000 miles away.

Babski believes a new generation has to stand firm on the small points and well as the big. "You need ethics," she said. "You don't flip the shot. A guy's mole is on his right cheek, not his left. These things ensure credibility so that people trust you. Just because someone didn't see you steal something doesn't mean you didn't do it. You have to be true to the story and not be pressured by lack of time or money. There are no shortcuts. You earn your luck by doing what good journalists have done for the last one hundred, two hundred years. You have to keep the rules sacred because journalism will not work otherwise."

For a different outlook, I went to Jim Bittermann, whose resume reads like alphabet soup. Since leaving the Waukegan News-Sun in Illinois, back in 1970, he worked abroad for CBS, ABC, and NBC before joining CNN in 1996. Based in France since 1980, he also teaches journalism at the American University in Paris. And that last part is a problem. It is hard to be optimistic for any but the brightest self-starters.

"You need survival instincts, the ability to
he said. "You have to get pictures that of   ....uning
above average and produce packages that stand out. It
was so easy when we started with large organizations that
had a brand. That was your reflected reputation. With
that ID card, you were taken as a trusted correspondent.
You can't do that anymore. You've got to figure out how
to develop your own personal brand."

Rather than target a single network, he says, a smarter
approach is to collect half a dozen strings, news outlets
that don't compete with each other. But that poses yet
another challenge: how to cast your stories. Each package
needs a universal appeal. Cultural references must be
explained. Remember that Japanese correspondent who
asked him to explain the Ten Commandments.

Bittermann advises young hopefuls to find an under-covered
capital and dig in. Places like Baghdad and Kabul are not
only dangerous but also full of eager stringers. He recom-
mends someplace like Athens or Madrid.

He is an old hand at conflict and crisis, but his forte
is the relaxed half-amused piece that tells people
so much about others. That is now a hard sell, even
for him.

"There is no room for the just-interesting story," he said,
"That has completely disappeared. People only get off
their chairs for something that is useful to them. People
used to come across things by accident, things that could
change their lives. That is the best thing about newspapers, just to be able to browse through them. We've going
to have less and less of this."

Bittermann is wide open to new ways, but he knows why
many of them cannot work. A former intern he trained,
now high in the ranks of Google, told him that investigative journalism and foreign reporting will come from the
street. The future is blogs by whistleblowers and others
who have direct access to the public. "But how do you

trust it?" he asked. "How do you find it? How do you know when to hit the bullshit button?"

As is usual for him, Bittermann ended on an up note. "You can be too negative about this," he said. "There are still people in the United States who read. I met a French guy the other day who works in computers, high-tech. He is reading a six-volume set of the history of France from 1340 to 1520 and the War of the Roses. Each is about six hundred pages." With people like that out there, he concludes, journalism has a future in all of its forms.

x

Radio, in its own particular way, can be more powerful than television, and it is much easier to crack. Networks no longer demand that correspondents find well-equipped studios; a clean cell phone signal is often good enough. Essential equipment is only a reliable sound recorder.

Few listeners realize how much skill and thought go into even the shortest radio piece. Like a newspaper dispatch, it needs a lead and a kicker, with characters, context, sources, facts, and a compelling tone. Capturing "actuality," those blaring horns, roaring crowds, and other audio imagery, is an undervalued specialty.

Like any other reporter, you need the ingenuity and audacity to get your microphone through closed doors or past armed goons. Mostly, you need to put people at ease and inspire their trust so they stay with you for questions that probe deeply.

Staff jobs are hard to find. Still, a resourceful freelancer undaunted by mud, bugs, and bill collectors can put together enough radio strings to survive. Start by using any particular advantage you might have: languages, cultural roots, or simple fascination. As in TV, find a place to start where occasional stories break and competition is scarce. However discouraging editors may be at the outset, when something pops you are worth gold.

Consider, for instance, Jamie Tarabay of NPR. She sees nothing daunting about this hard, lonely slog. That is how she started. As a Lebanese-Australian, she speaks Arabic and that antipodean flavor of English known as Strine. Combined with ferocious curiosity and a fearless nature, she pitched up in Israel and made friends at The Associated Press. We quickly saw the value, when heading into the West Bank and Gaza, of having her in the back seat.

After proving herself in Jerusalem, Tarabay moved to the AP bureau in Cairo and covered the Middle East. She liked doing radio spots and got good at them. When war turned ugly in Iraq, NPR recruited her. A stint at NPR in Washington taught her radio's specific skills.

"Sound is my adjective," Tarabay says. "It is easy to be descriptive in text. As a writer you can be incredibly evocative. In radio, you use sound to do that for you. I don't say, 'I'm standing on a crowded street.' You just hold out microphone to record the beeping horns, the cacophony of a market."

When I mentioned Cody's advice for word people – shut up and listen – she laughed. "That's exactly right. Never interrupt. If you stick a microphone in front of someone, they feel compelled to fill the air. If it stays there, they think, 'Obviously, she's not satisfied,' and they keep talking. The microphone says, 'That's not the answer I want, or you're avoiding the question, or you're giving me bullshit.'"

Tarabay sees a world of opportunity for new people in the business. Warmed up, she reeled off helpful advice for young journalists eager for a start in any medium. I just shut up and listened:

"The great thing about the Web is there are always people who will take your stuff, and you can get others to link to it. There are a thousand ways to get your name out there and show people what you can do. You have to make your product so good that someone will pay you something for it. You need something that distinguishes you from your competitors, something editors feel comfortable paying for that they're not going to get anyplace else.

"Before you go out, meet as many people as possible. Go to networks, talk to foreign editors. Of course, they won't give you a job. If you're going there on faith, they're not going to pay you. But at least when they see your email they're not going to delete it. It's only a matter of time if you're in a place where no one else is in, and they're going to say, wait, we've got someone. You might get only $150 for a day's work, but you get a connection. Plunk that in your CV and move on.

"Freelance is always a hassle, isn't it? The news industry is falling apart. Even AP is cutting down on actual reporters with these massive editing bureaus. This is a good opportunity to take advantage."

But, Tarabay cautioned, it is not so simple. She remembers the long nights she slept outside on stakeouts, such as when Israelis were about to bulldoze Yasser Arafat's compound, and days of treading lightly through mine fields. Getting close enough to the story to watch as it happens can be complex, dangerous work.

"You need the knowledge and the know-how. Some people say, 'I don't know anything about the place or the language, but I'll figure it out.' That's a really naïve approach. You've got to learn your street smarts and develop them. At the end of the day, we are documenting history. And if you have no concept of the background, you have no business being there."

Case Study Two

The Haiti Quake: How Does It Feel?

PAGE 154

Foreign correspondents once lamented that all their readers cared about were coups and earthquakes. Nowadays coups no longer stir much interest. But few stories get editors scurrying to deploy their troops like a powerful earthquake in a poor place, especially when it is only 700 miles south of Miami.

Interest is strong from sympathetic people who want to help. Some morbid curiosity figures in, with a trace of moralizing smugness: if those people had worked harder, built better houses, and believed in a respectable deity this would not have happened.

Reporters race in with mixed emotions. Many veterans hate covering earthquakes. Logistics are impossible. With only nature to blame, there are no villains to revile or underdogs to champion. Disheartening foul-ups and squabbles among relief agencies are inevitable. But then again, especially for TV correspondents, a lot of people are watching.

CNN pulled out all stops to cover the monster quake that collapsed much of Port-au-Prince and hinterlands beyond in January 2010. Plaudits came from Harry Evans, former London *Times* editor and grand old man of dead-trees-media, as well as Alessandra Stanley of *The New York Times*. Yet both tinged praise with the hard question: Where do you draw the line between reportage and self-promotion? Of all the praise, none was more effusive than what CNN heaped upon itself, with booming house-ad voices over images of muscular correspondents in tight dark T-shirts.

CNN, a short hop away in Atlanta, dispatched correspondents and crews quickly. Early coverage was understandably mixed. In disasters, intimate local knowledge is crucial so outsiders know how to help. Reporters who marvel at people sleeping outdoors in Port-au-Prince have clearly never been there before.

This was a star-power story. Anchors lamented repeatedly that Anderson Cooper was still en route. Soon he was in place, and so was the other heavy hitter, Dr. Sanjay Gupta. A quarter million people were dead, with uncounted others trapped under rubble and much of Haiti in ruins, but CNN focused on Gupta's medical ministrations. Other reporters overlooked the big picture for up-close emotion. Some seemed fixed on finding a photogenic victim as a personal prop. One thrust a microphone at an exhausted rescue worker and posed that question: "How does it feel?" The man scowled, "Not good."

In Paris at the time, I switched back and forth among CNN, the BBC, Al Jazeera, and France 24.

French reporters were too far away for immediate coverage, but they knew the background. Slaves founded Haiti by wresting it from France. As in most former French colonies, the elite studied in Paris, where deposed dictators scurried to safety.

Al Jazeera had only Mike Kirsch, a U.S.-based reporter who had worked in Miami and knew the Caribbean. On that crucial first day, I learned as much from him as from the whole CNN team. Keeping himself out of the picture, he focused on victims trapped in rubble but also survivors scrambling for water and scraps of food. Kirsch noted the U.S. military's essential role. But at Port-au-Prince airport, he showed troops unloading their own kit and setting up security perimeters as planes carrying relief supplies diverted to the Dominican Republic. The problem was plain: It was as if firemen had raced to a burning house and then stopped for lunch before turning on the hoses.

Al Jazeera was first to give a sense of the human cost, citing U.N. sources who estimated 200,000 people had died. Months later, the toll was established at above 230,000.

The BBC did a masterful job from the first hours. Its three U.S. correspondents, seasoned professionals, moved in close, but they refrained from coddling young victims. Matt Frei, who had done so well when Katrina struck New Orleans, found overlooked pockets of widespread devastation. He layered in rich texture, covering Haiti's tormented history, corruption-crippled economy, and all-suffering society. BBC cameras showed relief workers in Jacmel and other forgotten areas while nearly everyone else focused on the capital.

With Haiti still reeling, an earthquake struck Chile, 500

times more powerful on the Richter scale. The death toll was a fraction of Haiti's, but that was part of the story. Solid construction and disaster planning are vital in vulnerable regions. Chile's economy and infrastructure were devastated. In the first week, the Pew Research Center noted, broadcast news devoted 16 percent of its coverage to Chile. But the following week that fell to 2 percent. Haiti accounted for 27 percent when the tremor first struck and, three weeks later, 11 percent.

Partly, this is how cash-strapped networks operate these days; they pour resources into the biggest stories and skimp on the rest. But there is another phenomenon as old as journalism: Some places attract less interest than others. Generations ago, desk editors at a London newspaper competed to write what they considered to be the most boring deadline. Claud Cockburn won with, "Small Earthquake in Chile; Not Many Dead."

Chile is a long way off, but CNN found disaster drama it could cover from Atlanta: a tsunami headed toward Hawaii. Anchorman Rick Sanchez's grasp of the story was not comforting. Pointing out Hawaii on a map, he jabbed a finger at the Galapagos Islands. He badgered a scientist who tried to explain why there was no cause to panic over a 9-meter wave still far off in the South Pacific. Sanchez demanded to know how high that was in English. When told the answer, 27 feet, he grew yet more agitated. And so on.

When the online mockery died down, Sanchez went on the air with a half-amused apology for the question about meters – "Stupid me" – but he found a viewer's email that claimed the metric system was French, not English. He said he was called in unprepared and was perhaps a little hard on his guest.

For all of CNN's good work in Haiti, the overall picture was disturbing. Serious journalism is measured by consistency and depth over time. Jon Stewart delivered the coup de grace: "See, that's the thing about news in a disaster. You need the information fast and inaccurate."

Photographers: Beyond Snappers

chapter eleven

Correspondents have given themselves a nickname, hacks, and I don't much like it. True, we should take our work seriously but not ourselves. Yet it is an old term for writers who grind out drivel, and there are so many of the other kind. The photographers' equivalent, snappers, carries no negative baggage. We all know that clicking a shutter is a small part of something much bigger.

The two used to be separate categories at news agencies and big dailies. Writers assumed the upper hand. Photographers were there to illustrate their stories. They had to hang around during interviews, missing other pictures. When action was fierce, they worked all day and stayed up half the night to process film and send pictures. Reporters could watch from a safe distance and get details later from someone else, such as their photographer.

This began to change in the 1990s with a new approach at The Associated Press. Editors wanted their photographers to find pictures that told stories of their own. At first, transition was difficult. Free at last, photographers shunned what were derisively termed "story illustrations." But some stories need illustration. This got ugly once when I profiled an aid worker in the Congo, and no one wanted to waste time taking a mere portrait. A balance worked itself out.

These days, the term reporter (or the French version: reporter) ought to cover snappers as well as hacks. Exhibit A is Gary Knight, a substantially built Briton. He went to Southeast Asia in the 1980s. Penniless at first, he quickly made his mark. After shooting for *Newsweek* and others, he enlisted a handful of top freelancers and set up the VII Photo Agency (www.viiphoto.com). In 2009, he took a Nieman fellowship at Harvard to study ancient Rome and more modern empires.

Knight and I co-edited the quarterly, *Dispatches*, with a common view: journalists are journalists. "You're not there to make pretty pictures," Knight said. He brushes aside questions of gear and technology, which go quickly obsolete. "It's about how to tell the truth, motivation, and ethics. It's a question of how to be an excellent journalist, irrespective of whether you're writing or photographing, or even Twittering if that's the only way to get the story. That is what distinguishes professionals from bloggers."

x

For me, a sea change came in 1990 as I planned a trip across Soviet Central Asia. I had ached to get to Samarkand and beyond, mostly off limits to journalists. The idea was to play tourist, then dig deep when that seemed smart. My editor insisted that I take a photographer. I balked. It would be hard enough to go unnoticed without a sidekick toting gear. But I went with Greg English, an easy-going pro with sharp senses. His lenses told stories I could not, and he took us places I would have missed on my own.

When I mapped out an African trip to cover AIDS, I lobbied for a Norwegian photographer, insane in all the right ways, who knew the story well; he had suggested it. But New York insisted I take a young French hotshot named Jerome Delay, just hired in Washington from Agence France-Presse. After a week, I saw that in the peculiar math of global reporting one plus one can equal three. Over the next 15 years, our Froggy & Gonzo duo racked up front-page play from the Balkans, the Middle East, Asia, and Africa.

Near Sarajevo, I was noting down a woman's harrowing story when Jerome caught my eye from 50 yards away. He made a subtle nod. I cut off my interview as politely as I could and bolted off in his direction. He had pictured an old woman on her knees scooping up dirt in a courtyard. I spoke no Serbo-Croatian, but she knew Italian.

"Once I was a lady," she began. I already had a lead. Destitute, she fed her children by selling bits of brass from spent cartridges. "People tell me I might get killed doing this," she told me. "So far, I haven't been that lucky." With a compelling portrait of the woman's hands in the dirt and words to go with it, the story made front pages across the world.

Later, as Kosovars crossed into Albania in wagons pulled by putt-putt tractors, I gave Jerome a similar nod. He hurried over and caught a row of tiny kids peeking out from under a tarp, a vignette that cut through all complexity.

For starters, Jerome is a photographer of stunning talent, with a craftsman's mastery of his tools and an artist's sense for visual power. But more, he is a reporter who understands what is important and what resonates with people half a world away.

After every burst of the shutter, he stops to take names and ask questions. Each subject is a real person, part of a larger story. When things calmed in Sarajevo, I went back with him to track down people he had photographed during the worst of the war.

Hajrudin Sejdic, the 9-year-old kid on Gypsy Hill, was gone forever. He lined up for water one morning, as he always did, and the Egyptian Army truck with a U.N. flag accidentally ran him over. We found his grave. Nihad Vrago, who found fame leaping onto the roof of his burning house, chuckled at the memory. At the time, no one knew why. "I was after our little fortune, money and gold," he explained. "I don't want to say how much burned up in that damned fire. It hurt." We had trouble finding Mujesira Jusufovic, pictured as she hung laundry on a bombed-out balcony. She was penniless in a hovel across town. "At least we're alive," she said. "Thank God for that."

Unlike writers, photographers have no way around that basic dictum of being there. Words allow a lot of leeway. But if you do not make the picture, no amount of fancy footwork can cover you.

"No" and "can't" are not in Jerome's lexicon. I treasure his portrait of a Tuareg sheik in a blue turban, burnt-copper face reflecting rich red tones of the hangings in his tent. We had gone to Mali to report on drought and met a U.N. official in the capital, Bamako. The man had just visited that Tuareg who, propelled by a vision, led his band to a desolate sand dune 100 miles northwest of Timbuktu. "It's a shame you weren't with me," the U.N. man told us. "You could never find him." Jerome and I exchanged glances. He made that portrait barely 24 hours later.

We raced to the airport, lucked onto an infrequent flight to Timbuktu, and found a Land Cruiser with a U.N. driver and several trigger-happy soldiers to ward off bandits. As these things happen, it was a story that told the story.

×

Any Jerome Delay exploit is a primer in itself for photographers on the road. Sometimes, we broke major news. Other times, I went along as the Froggy & Gonzo caption writer. He called one morning, excited. The first round-the-world balloon trip was about to end somewhere in North Africa. I'm not much for balloons, but he is. We got a map.

Breitling, the watchmaker sponsor in Switzerland, was saying nothing. Its public-relations team set up a charter flight for a chosen few. A recovery jeep would meet the two balloonists, and access would be carefully controlled.

Clearly, we reasoned, showmen traveling by hot air would head for the pyramids near Cairo. But wind currents are tricky. We bought plane tickets to Cairo and Luxor but also Marrakech and Rabat in Morocco as well as Bamako. As the balloon crossed Africa, it seemed headed for Cairo. I flew there, but Jerome's editor in New York ordered him to wait. He wasn't much on balloons, either.

At midnight, hundreds of reporters milled around the control center at Giza, each with hired cars, taxis, and minivans. The landing site would be an oasis 200 miles to the southwest in nearly trackless desert. Jerome finally got a go-ahead from New York; his plane arrived at 3 a.m. By 4:30, he had persuaded the guy in charge to take us along in the recovery vehicle, a Toyota Land Cruiser fitted out for Saharan rallies. The hitch was that he could not bring us back. No problem. We'd figure it out.

Before dawn, the Toyota roared off, leaving the pack in billowing dust. The driver, an Egyptian rally champion, chuckled sympathetically and goosed it. As we sped along the Nile, he apologized. He would have to leave us at the airstrip near the oasis while he picked up the balloonists. Hours later, the Toyota screeched to a halt.

"We're lost," the leader said.

"No, we're not," Jerome said. He extracted a GPS he had bought at Amsterdam Airport, the first one any of us had ever seen. He pinpointed our location and plotted out a route across barely visible camel tracks.

The Egyptian looked longingly at the GPS.

"It's yours if you get us to the balloon," Jerome said. At that, the guy produced headscarves and welcomed us to the crew; we were mechanics.

Soon, the Toyota stopped again. The driver heard on the radio that the landing site would be somewhere else. Jerome fired up a prototype satellite phone he had raided from the AP Paris bureau. "Here," he said. "Call Geneva." We were assured the plan had not changed.

When we reached the oasis and waited to join the short convoy going to meet the balloon, a photographer in the official pool busted us. The convoy left us behind, disconsolate. Then we learned the Egyptian Air Force had changed signals. A helicopter fetched the balloonists as soon as they landed. Minutes after the official convoy sped away, Bertrand Piccard and Brian Jones touched down at the oasis. Jerome's exclusive picture, with both men holding their clasped hands aloft, became the cover of *National Geographic*.

A press charter from Cairo arrived just then, and a gaggle of reporters rushed up to shout questions. I yelled a question in French. Piccard, relieved to hear his own tongue, answered at length. By the time he switched to English, Jerome had already sent pictures around the world and dictated my scribbled urgent arrival story to an editor. When the questions stopped, I asked Piccard if he wanted to call his wife. He did. After finishing on Jerome's phone, he relaxed for a leisurely interview.

Soon, the press flight was ready to return to Cairo. Jerome was still filing. I stalled the plane, inventing problems and excuses until the captain put his foot down. Jerome's last pictures had not cleared. I could not leave him behind, and I dreaded a return to Cairo by camel. But he flew up the stairs just as they began to roll back.

Early the next morning, we were back in Paris, 30 or so hours after Jerome had reached Cairo.

×

As big as the world is, the community of top-flight photographers is surprisingly small. Most know each other well. And all of them know something about everyone else's work. Partly, this is a sign of how thinly "the media" covers global news. But more, it is because serious practitioners share triumphs and frustrations in an imperiled profession.

When Knight started shooting for *Newsweek*, two or three photographers were assigned to big stories. They arrived well in advance of the magazine's Friday deadline, up to 10 days early if the subject might lead the issue. These days, a single photographer has only a few days to fly in, scope out the story, and make pictures. A skilled hand can produce images in a short time, but that leaves no time for the reporting that gives images meaning.

In this community, there is sometimes treachery. Photographers still talk about the first days of Romania's revolution, in 1989, when they all sent their film to Paris with a colleague. He managed to lose everyone's but his own. Earlier in Beirut, two close friends, both French, pooled resources and shared a room. Their driver woke one to say 241 U.S. Marines had been blown up. He rushed off without waking his friend.

More often, there is a great generosity. Soon after the Serbs fled Kosovo, Knight was in Prizren with James Nachtwey, who was working for the competition, *Time*. As their deadlines approached, they planned to drive out together to Macedonia where they could ship negatives. A day before leaving, Nachtwey told Knight about a picture he had made, the ghostly imprint of a body pressed into the dirt, a powerful image that perfectly caught the sense of the story. Nachtwey waited 24 hours so Knight could go make a similar photo.

Later, the two joined other grand photographers to form their own agency, VII. Essentially, it was a case of the lunatics taking over the asylum. Each had worked with large agencies — Magnum, Saba, SIPA, and others — that marketed their pictures but kept a hefty cut.

Even more than word people, photographers ready to work hard, get close, and suffer through tough times can make their names in today's new climate. It is easy for editors to overlook or plunder a freelancer's superlative piece of writing. A hard-won quote set artfully within intelligent context is quickly forgotten. But a brilliant photo carries an immediate impact, and it lives on. One or two of these might be luck. When they regularly occur, editors notice and ask you for more.

Internships can help. In journalism, one should be care-ful about these. Companies love the idea of free or cheap labor and use as much of it as they can. This can be exploitative, wasting valuable time for young people when they are open to fresh experiences and lessons learned on their own. If internships lead to something, they are beyond worth it. With photography, they can be crucial.

But these are strange times. When Nicholas Kristof of *The New York Times* invites young people to join him on the road, thousands apply with pleading letters. In 2009, an assistant posted an intern job on Nachtwey's website. A deluge of virulent hate mail excoriated him for trying to weasel free labor. Some admitted they had never seen his work. Many were incoherent and illiterate. They failed to see the opportunity here. For photogra-phers, the best place to start is at the feet of a master.

Although no one can make it without skill and drive, few fields of endeavor depend so heavily on who you know. For beginners, getting a swamped editor to glance at their work is already a triumph. Many promising hopefuls go unnoticed until they run out of capital and give up.

A season spent with any VII-quality professional opens doors that slam shut to the uninvited and imparts superior technical knowledge. Consider, for instance, Christopher Morris, among the best war photographers of our time. He interned with Jim Nachtwey and then joined him at *Time*.

Basic training for photojournalists is essentially the same as for those in any medium. Learn the world from the bottom up, from early history to last week's headlines. Focus on the individual humans who make up humanity. Find a place that interests you, without impossible competition, and go to work.

But there is more. Understand the rules and follow them. Do not fake a photo. You might make a dramatic picture by, say, getting a Bosnian cellist drunk, dressing him in tails, and taking him to a cemetery as an evocative backdrop. But your colleagues will know.

Resist Photoshop temptations. A Reuters photographer once blackened smoke columns rising over Beirut after an Israeli bombing raid. His place in history is not the one he was after.

Study work you admire and get to know who did it. Word people can be hard to pin down, but most photographers are not. Don't email. Go in person in exhibitions and talks. Photo shows are often mob scenes, and making useful contacts takes some luck. Persist. But, as with making good pictures, luck depends on being in the places where luck happens.

×

The greatest challenge is feeling the human empathy that touches people somewhere down deep. Young photographers reared comfortably in America and Europe might quickly master basic skills. Many produce beautifully composed, technically perfect work. But capturing the sudden death of war, or the slower death of desperate poverty, takes more than that.

When Gary Knight judges the World Press Photo contest in Amsterdam, he paws through thousands of pictures, spending a split second on each until something stops him. He is disheartened by so many of the war photos that convey so little.

"My generation lived under the Cold War, and I grew up as a child knowing that one day I would be annihilated," he said. "An earlier generation lived through World War II. This one has no point of view, with little political or intellectual to add to discussion. War is bad. People get killed. Thanks, we know that. They are neither for nor against, and the storytelling is weak."

When he teaches, Knight shows students how photographers in Vietnam approached their work. Larry Burrows focused steadily more closely on the human cost, which turned *Life* magazine away from the war. David Douglas Duncan, a Marine colonel at Iwo Jima in World War II, championed the troops. Philip Jones Griffiths, a Welch nationalist who empathized with Vietnamese victims, came down like a sledgehammer. AP's Horst Faas won his Pulitzer for pictures about people, soldiers and civilians alike.

"Now it is often like looking at a postcard or a painting, and that doesn't educate the public," Knight concluded. "That, for me, is the difference between Vietnam and now."

War Reporting:
Vietraqistan

chapter twelve

In the humbling aftermath of Vietnam, many Americans missed the lesson they paid so heavily to learn: in war, journalists are as vital as medics, and they need similar access to frontlines. People back home have to know how, and why, blood is spilled in their name. When war ends, generals can fade away and write their books. But an entire nation must face the inevitable global consequences.

Armies are made up of individuals, many good, some bad, and a few downright evil. Officers study Clausewitz. Reporters would do better with *Lord of the Flies*; even decent young soldiers go rogue. With the best of intentions, things can get horribly strange. Commanders and grunts alike must be held to account.

Generals, understandably, resist such scrutiny. Journalists littering their battlefields can be a major pain. More than that, military commanders need an esprit de corps to keep troops jazzed under life-and-death circumstances. Dispatches that reveal failed missions and low morale, let alone atrocities, weaken public support.

Epitomizing the past is risky. Things were seldom as they seem from distant hindsight. Yet the Vietnam War is a landmark by which to measure how far we have come in the wrong direction.

After Vietnam, the U.S. military curbed "media personnel" by restricting access. News organizations, rather than pushing back collectively, competed to jump into pools and climb into "embeds." Briefings were once gritty give-and-take between reporters and field officers. Now, televised with fancy graphic on elaborate sound stages, they play directly to a sympathetic citizenry.

Courageous reporters manage to reflect hard reality from Iraq and Afghanistan. But if the military sometimes helps, it is often an obstacle. And, when reporters are within range of over-amped young gunners spoiling for a fight, it can be downright dangerous.

Stray friendly fire is a hazard to everyone, a risk of any war. But journalists have been killed pointblank when they were clearly no threat. Stuff happens, yes. But too many questions go unasked and unanswered.

The Pentagon keeps close tabs on its troops. Some after-action reports are classified because they might aid the enemy. Yet others are kept secret only because they are embarrassing if not incriminating. Editors can file Freedom of Information Act requests, and generals can tell them to go pound sand.

Although reporters in combat zones assume the risks, commanders must do what they can to minimize those risks. When this last part is ignored, truth — always an early casualty in war — barely has a fighting chance.

Military structures include people with consciences, and ugly realities sometimes surface. In April 2010, leaked gun-camera video showed a harrowing incident in Baghdad. Response to it — by U.S. officials, by news organizations, and by the public at large — said much about how the Pentagon-Press balance has shifted since Vietnam.

×

In a 17-minute short version of the video, millions of people from Akron to Ahmadabad watched a U.S. Army Apache helicopter spray .30 caliber rounds at 12 unarmed people as they walked casually down a Baghdad street. It looked very much like wanton slaughter. Victims included Namir Noor-Eldeen, a Reuters cameraman with a lens slung over his shoulder, and his driver, Saeed Chmagh. Noor-Eldeen was only wounded at first. A gunner stitched him with bullets as he crawled to safety.

Had the killings been inadvertent, the Army might have explained and apologized. But when the video was taken, in July 2007 from a second Apache, briefers described the victims as armed combatants. Apparently insurgents had been active in that area earlier so anyone there was assumed to be the enemy. For three years, the Pentagon stonewalled Reuters' repeated FOIA requests to see the footage.

Eventually, an inside source passed the gun-camera video to Wikileaks.org, a group of journalists-turned-advocates whose posts break stories no one else reports. Experts helped to decrypt it.

U.S. Defense Secretary Robert Gates said the video was taken out of context and distorted reality. Many people, with little faith in the Pentagon's credibility, preferred to trust their own eyes and ears. And, later, the gunners apologized.

The scene is immediately clear to anyone with a notion of conflict situations. A small group ambles in plain sight down the middle of the street, unconcerned by two Apache gunships just overhead. Even on small computer screens, the camera slung over Noor-Eldeen's shoulder does not look menacing. The view would have been better from overhead.

One gunner says he sees "individuals with AK-47s." That would have been a minimal threat. A Kalashnikov is a Model T Ford, an assault rifle designed for close-range combat. An Apache gunship, agile as Harry Potter's quidditch broom, can fire 625 rounds a minute.

A voice adds, "He's got an RPG." An armed rocket-propelled grenade launcher is four feet long and unmistakable. It is hard to imagine anyone dumb enough to aim one in plain site of two Apaches.

The gunners seem itching for any excuse to shoot, like excited kids at a video game. One pleads for permission to engage until a voice says, "Light 'em all up." After intense fire punctuated by triumphant whoops, a gunner spots one victim trying to crawl away. It is Noor-Eldeen. Into his mike, he taunts him to reach for a weapon. The gunner decides that is the case — with no weapon in sight — and he blasts away.

A van races up to evacuate casualties, and it is laced with bullets. Men on the ground find a wounded young girl inside.

"Well, it's their fault for bringing kids into a battle," a voice says.

"That's right," another adds.

x

After a brief flurry of attention, the video faded into the shadows. *The New York Times* did a piece on Wikileaks and another on how American soldiers are taught to dehumanize potential targets so they don't lose their edge. An AP dispatch summed up the story's elements, saying that it was old news with a fresh twist.

One of my smartest students at Arizona offered a troubling assessment. The video was biased, she said, because of its passionate profile of the dead Reuters cameraman. It was not an objective source, and it besmirched America's fighting men.

Passion, if not outrage, drives most useful sources in conflict coverage. A reporter has to look beyond motive to the substance beneath. Quotes from passionate advocates must be handled carefully, set into careful context. What counts is whether the information they unearth is solid.

Insiders who leaked the Pentagon Papers were hardly objective. *The New York Times*, satisfied with their authenticity, defied the government and published them at length. That altered the course of the Vietnam War.

x

In World War II, correspondents wore uniforms and mostly ignored civilians as no more than garnish on the plate. Correspondents in Korea focused narrowly on military matters. No one noted that U.S. troops mowed down refugees by the hundreds near the bridge at No Gun Ri, an atrocity far beyond the scope of My Lai in Vietnam. Charles Hanley and AP colleagues finally dug out the facts from Pentagon records and interviews with veterans nearly two generations later.

Vietnam's American War was different. It began slowly in

the early 1960s as a shadow play. Covert U.S. agents tried to channel political currents remaining from France's earlier debacle. Then military "advisers" helped South Vietnam in battle. Before long, all-out war pitted Americans against Viet Cong guerrillas and North Vietnamese regulars who streamed down along the Ho Chi Minh Trail.

As a story, it had everything: a corrupt ruling class, complete with dragon lady; evil Communists; ancient cultures in an exotic setting; steamy nights of sin after long days of invigorating danger; exotically good local food with extra French flavor.

And it was the sixties. Some young people, American and otherwise, wanted to add adventure to the usual grind of sex, drugs, and rock and roll. Others saw a chance to dig deep into a story of far-reaching consequences. Richard Nixon had gotten America to look outward. John F. Kennedy and Lyndon Johnson were holding the line against Communism.

Those daily briefings, immortalized as the Five O'Clock Follies, were blunt exchanges between military officers and the working press. No one played to a public gallery. When one captain droned on with useless drivel, Jay Caldwell of AP interrupted. "Sir," he said, "tell us about instances of self-abuse among B52 pilots." When Joe Fried of the New York *Daily News* demanded details of some distant action, the briefer replied, "We'd be happy to take you there." The room exploded with laughter. Fried, everyone knew, never left Saigon.

Most reporters covered Vietnam the hard way. They got close to field commanders and firebase grunts. In between, they ate at noodle stalls and visited the Cholon morning market to buy back gear stolen from them the night before. Some married into Saigon society, and others settled for late nights in raucous bars.

Late in 2009, Richard Holbrooke sparked some fury when he remarked, "The terrible truth that people do not like to admit was that the (Vietnam) war was fun if they were civilians or journalists." Burying friends or getting caught in heavy fire is not that amusing. Yet some of it was fun.

The Vietnam War created such a bond among journalists that when a lovably curmudgeon photographer named Hugh Van Es died in 2009, several hundred rallied to a Google group they called Vietnam-Old-Hacks. They exchanged stories, resolved forgotten mysteries, and harangued one another with precise detail. My inbox contains more than 1,000 posts.

Looking back, most agreed on main points. Today's new technology would have made reporting more convenient but not more complete. Old hands regretted not using their unfettered access to dig deeper into what the war was really about, how it affected the Vietnamese, and why it could not have been won.

In April 2010, a revolving reunion began in Vientiane, Laos, and moved on to Phnom Penh before a final tour of Vietnam. Local reporters covered them like rock stars. I am pretty certain that so long after the Iraq War ends, if it ever does, aging correspondents will not fill the Palestine Hotel to reminisce over high times on the Tigris.

×

So much has been written about Vietnam that it is pointless to dwell on it here. But it is important to understand how different it was from today.

Reporters went wherever they were crazy enough to go. Officers, they found, are usually more helpful the closer they are to the action. Old hands helped each other, sharing contacts and insights. Even casual stringers had an equivalent rank of major for priority on aircraft. Editors and executives backed their people on the ground, and they insisted on access however much the Pentagon objected.

"The press never had it that good before, hasn't since and probably never will again," Richard Pyle replied when I asked him to compare then and now. After running AP's Saigon bureau, he made a specialty of covering Americans at war. "The access we had to the battlefield and the freedom to report, free of restrictions including formal censorship, was unprecedented. But because that war was lost, the press was readily and falsely blamed by a lot of resentful military people."

It is more important still to understand what has not changed. In Vietnam, as in Afghanistan and Iraq, reporters who risked their lives to witness news firsthand were often overshadowed by punditry from Washington.

Home-front commentary can add important dimensions, yet distance always distorts. Dispatches from the field reveal situations of dizzying intricacy. We need to know these nuances, the human detail, and those seemingly small political wrinkles from which the big story depends. Without all of this, world-shaping conflict becomes meaningless generality, the war in Vietraqistan.

x

As overt war took shape in Vietnam, a handful of young reporters quickly saw what Americans were up against. But a few influential columnists with little notion of guerrilla tactics, or Indochina, attacked them as naïve leftists. As the war escalated so did the press corps. Washington commentators saw lights at the end of tunnels, which were not visible at close hand.

Forty years later, during the run-up to Iraq, a similar drama played out. Reporters on the spot wrote what they saw. Editors back home, reflecting views of their own Washington sources and their own impressions from television, told them what they should be seeing.

From Jordan, anyone with Saigon experience could see Vietnam similarities all over the place. Iraq was sand, not jungle. Marsh Arabs were not Annamese. But France and the United States had both paid heavily to learn that ancient peoples resist foreigners who shoot their way in to reorganize things according to their own plan.

My own experience reflected that of others. I tracked down military officers and civilians I had known in Vietnam. All saw the same dangers. When I wrote this for AP, it was spiked. One editor explained, "We think it is too early to talk about Vietnam."

Reporters in Baghdad, closer to the story, saw what was coming. Religious leaders reminded them of the British invasion after World War I. Sunni and Shia fought side-by-side, gathering in each other's mosques, to turn back a common foe. Britain spent two years failing to subdue Iraq. U.N. inspectors made clear they had no evidence of the chemical, biological weapons, or nuclear precursors that justified an invasion.

When Barack Obama turned Washington's attention back to Afghanistan, reporters hurried in from every direction. And it was, in Yogi Berra-speak, déjà vu all over again. Young reporters with a fresh take on the story joined old hands with hard experience to cover the war in person. But, these days, anyone with a computer can have a say, even if they can't find Helmand Province on a map. As in the past, a Greek chorus in Washington narrated its perceived reality in the background.

x

The first priority in making sense of any conflict is to find trustworthy informants. Smart reporters quickly determine who to tap for background guidance. Smart readers, viewers, and listeners can do the same by singling out reporters whose work rings true. Whether they articulate well is far less important than whether they know what they're talking about.

The much-maligned "corporate media" fields some exceedingly skilled professionals. Most have "locals" on their staffs with solid contacts and an insider's feel for the story.

The mainstream also deploys plenty of the other kind. As U.S. troops stormed toward Baghdad from Kuwait, I nearly threw blunt objects at the TV screen whenever CNN aired one familiar old hand embedded with them. He enthused about his Humvee, Betsy, but largely ignored the dead Iraqi civilians in the convoy's wake.

What counts is the journalist, not the employer. Edward Girardet, who contributes to *The Christian Science Monitor*, among others, first sneaked into Afghanistan with resistance forces in 1979. By 2010, he had made more than 80 trips. Over platters of lamb and rice or under fire, he got to know every warlord who matters. From Geneva, he publishes the indispensable *Field Guide to Afghanistan*.

War attracts a full gamut, from serious reporters anxious to ride along with history to headbangers: runners and gunners addicted to thrills if not something more. The latter might produce more insight and eyewitness reality than the former. In both cases, readers who do not recognize their names cannot assess their credibility.

In Vietnam, freelancers needed an outlet — an agency, a newspaper or magazine, a network — for their dispatches and photos. This created filters. Crazies and fabulists were shunned, and the good ones learned journalistic ethics. This also gave them the authority of whatever news organization carried their work. Today, anyone can declare himself, or herself, a war correspondent.

News consumers need to apply suspended belief. If something seems too odd to be true, check it. It probably isn't true. Then again, it just might be. The Internet that brings us so many untested amateurs also enables us to check on who they are and what they have said in the past.

People who care about reality can learn over time who can provide it for them, fairly and incisively. With a firm grasp of how war reporting works, anyone can add enough grains of salt to put together a reasonably clear picture.

×

Traditional news organizations are equipped to cover war from three essential vantage points. We can call these Big Picture, Soda Straw, and Free Range.

Big Picture is obvious and inevitable. Most of us see only those choreographed "news conferences" in Washington or at command headquarters, with misleading imagery to engage a wider public. So many reporters crowd in that briefers can focus on friendly ringers and stonewall the over-informed and obstreperous. Remember how Donald Rumsfeld mocked those who questioned his Iraq optimism while a sympathetic claque chortled?

Off camera, however, serious journalists dig deep. Their sources include top officers with private doubts, and staff people who leak crucial data. Those scorned "hotel journalists" in Kabul and Iraq play a vital role, smoking out hidden strategies and nailing official lies. They can follow up on field reports and make contacts within the factions around which conflict turns.

Soda Straw reporting allows a close-up look with a narrow range of vision. It is the most popular type, ranging from the vivid vignettes Ernie Pyle wrote in World War II to today's flow of Hi-Mom puff pieces beloved by media executives and Pentagon flacks. They sell papers, boost ratings, and engage citizens who pay for the war. They guarantee footage, photos, and quotes. For strategists who studied Vietnam, embedding is a perfect soda straw. It offers the access a democracy demands while corralling hordes of journalists who might otherwise clutter up the battlefield. Officials can vet candidates and direct their line of sight.

Some soda-straw reporting is deftly done, adding insight we would otherwise miss. Good journalists know when they are being conned, and they find ways to elude the watchful eye. In the heat of battle, no one bothers with them. But the limits are severe. When you race forward in armored

vehicles, you cannot stop to interview people in the bloody
wreckage you leave behind.

Free Range reporting is the hardest to do and the most
difficult for readers to evaluate. And it is, by far, the
most important. What the Pentagon called "unilaterals"
in the first Gulf War are now "non-embeds." These are
synonyms for journalists doing what they should be able
to do in any story: finding action as it happens, staying
long enough to talk with people, and returning to headquarters to demand answers to what they know to be
the crucial questions.

This can be extremely dangerous work, as the Wikileak.org
video shows. Nervous kids with serious weaponry, committed to "force protection," fire freely at anything
that seems out of place. Gunners and pilots make mistakes.
"Media personnel" roaming around loose are a major nuisance
to commanders. To some, they amount to the enemy. The
Pentagon has yet to convince Al Jazeera or Reuters
executives that casualties their people suffered in Iraq
were not in some way deliberate.

x

The first Gulf War, with its doctrine of overwhelming
force, rewrote the old rules. Col. David Hackworth, a
much-decorated officer, wrote for *Newsweek* in 1991: "I
had more guns pointed at me by Americans or Saudis who
were into controlling the press than in all my years of
actual combat. We didn't have the freedom of movement
to make an independent assessment of what the military
is all about."

Having seen war at its worst, Hackworth knows. We all felt
the same. My only experience as a prisoner of war in 40
years of reporting was at the hands of Gen. Barry
McCaffery's 24th Infantry Division near the Iraqi border.
In Dhahran, allergic to pools, I heard that any "unilaterals"
able to find McCaffrey's forward positions could stay
until the invasion started. A photographer and I followed

a trail of broken-down 24th Division tanks awaiting repair. A crewman gave us general directions. Then we found a clue: a sign pointed to "Hinesville" as though Iraqi spies would not know where the division based in Georgia.

As we approached the command center, military police detained us. We said we would return to Dhahran. They told us not to leave until a public affairs officer came to yell at us. If we did, they added, they would shoot. A captain arrived and advised, "You're in deep shit." I said that unless I had missed a military coup in Washington, he was in deep shit. We were civilians.

When his colonel eventually drove up, I started yelling first. He directed us back to Dhahran under our own recognizance. The U.S. information chief told the Saudi liaison officer our visas should be revoked. He laughed. "Sir," he said, "haven't you read your First Amendment?"

I had been on McCaffrey's hit list. Months before, I was escorted to the division's rear base for what public affairs officers expected to be patriotic puffery. Heavy weaponry was in such bad shape, with field armor able to move only in reverse, that I chose not to write about it. Instead, I reported on the soldiers' states of mind, and it was decided that I was not on the team.

Earlier, James LeMoyne of *The New York Times* had a shouting match with McCaffery's aides who tried to direct what he wrote. It was plain where the general stood on how "media personnel" should function. Years later, CNN hired McCaffery as a military analyst to comment on coverage of Iraq and Afghanistan.

The best work was by reporters who stayed clear of pools and headquarters. It was easier then because a true coalition offered options. One AP colleague found the French Foreign Legion up near the border. Officers showed him around and briefed him on their armament. Tell Saddam what we've got, one of them said, and that we're waiting.

But this was a sorry shadow of Vietnam. When I returned to one outpost, the commander scowled. The Pentagon had tracked down soldiers I quoted and punished them – and him. Back home, neither editors nor executives seemed to care.

"Segments of the press have already surrendered to the military minders," Leon Daniel of UPI observed in Dhahran. He was on his last hurrah after a career that started in the early years of Vietnam. "What you have is what the shrinks call the Stockholm syndrome."

Christiane Amanpour, just starting out with CNN, added, "If we happen to stumble across news, we can't use it because it has to be cleared." Generals could not have hoped in their wildest dreams for such favorable publicity before the war, she said. "Now suddenly we are the enemy."

When the Gulf War ended, Jacqueline Sharkey compiled a report, *Under Fire*, for the Center for Public Integrity. Then head of the University of Arizona's journalism department, she made her bones with the *Washington Post* and as an independent reporter. In 1990, she foresaw the upset victory of Violeta Chamorro as Nicaraguan president. Almost everyone else predicted Daniel Ortega and his Sandinistas would win again. Sharkey listened to real people.

Sharkey documented how the Pentagon's media policies evolved since Vietnam. American news executives sought the illusion of access rather than the real thing. The White House and Pentagon savaged the Bill of Rights. Few citizens objected.

During the bungled invasion of Grenada and the overthrow of Gen. Manuel Noriega in Panama officers herded reporters into holding areas. Some objected loudly, but without a common voice. As plans were laid to invade Kuwait, American and foreign reporters had to fight among themselves for limited spaces in pools that would go where officers decided to send them.

When one pool went to the edge of Khafji, the Saudi border

town Iraqis briefly held, an NBC-TV reporter spotted Robert Fisk of the London *Independent*. He had gotten into Khafji for a hard look around on his own. Fisk wrote that the NBC man shouted obscenities and yelled: "You'll prevent us from working. You're not allowed here. Get out. Go back to Dhahran." Alerted, the pool escort forbade Fisk from talking to Marines.

Officers vetted copy and sometimes changed it. Frank Bruni, then with the *Detroit Free Press*, described troops as giddy. That became, proud. Another reporter mentioned beer, which evaporated from his copy.

Sharkey concluded:

"The sad truth is that while reporters and editors complained about the media restrictions, in the end many of them presented precisely the data and images that the White House and Defense Department wanted the press to pass along to the American people."

Frank Aukofer, the *Milwaukee Journal's* Washington bureau chief, gave Sharkey his own conclusion:

"We should not expect anything different in the future. When the crunch comes, military people become soldiers first and public affairs specialists somewhere behind that. Everything is subverted to the military objectives. All the good-faith planning in the world will not change that."

Aukofer was right about what to expect. Some believe that Round Two, the war in Iraq, provided more access because of embedding. But First Amendment notwithstanding, it was once again the Pentagon's show.

Perhaps more than anyone, Malcolm Browne of *The New York Times* saw the continuum change from the early 1960s in Vietnam to the early 1990s in the Gulf. As AP Saigon bureau chief, he got out to see the war in its human context. He was there with a camera when a Buddhist monk doused himself with gasoline and flicked a cigarette lighter. He kept a withered hand pinned to his office wall so reporters would not forget that they were writing about actual people. He pushed hard for access at every level and earned officers' respect.

When it was over, he said reporters had become unpaid employees of the Department of Defense.

The lesson for journalists and citizens is the same. In any democracy, press freedom is fundamental. From the head of state on down, public officials and military officers must answer to citizens. They can impose barriers only when citizens don't object.

During the first Gulf War, Gen. Colin Powell brushed aside complaints. History, he said, would sort out the truth. But history seldom sorts out truth. Reporters need to get it right the first time around.

Gen. Frederick Weyand, in command when the Vietnam War ended, defended reporters in an interview with *Vietnam* magazine in 1988. Some got things wrong, he said, but he looked at the larger picture. "I never subscribed to the simple-minded notion that the media lost the Vietnam War. I think most of the war correspondents in Vietnam were competent and capable professionals ... The media wields such great influence in shaping public opinion that it must be especially careful to get the story straight. The American people deserve at least that."

For that, reporters need access to reality.

x

There is a second and equally difficult challenge: To tell it like it really is. During the Bosnian war, Martin Bell of the BBC had all the access to reality he needed. Reporters in Balkans, mostly, managed to get anywhere they had the guts to go. But Bell's editors wanted no blood on the air before 9 p.m. and very little after that.

American networks are equally squeamish unless the blood is only part of an entertainment show about, say, a serial killer, like Dexter. Newspapers and magazines have their own guidelines to avoid shocking susceptible readers.

This is a problem. War, as we have all heard, is hell. If only the people who fight it or suffer from it feel its impact, it is needlessly repeated. It may shock a child to see pictures of white phosphorus searing the flesh of other children his age. But that is what happens. Should he grow up seeing war as a computer game in which casualties spring back to life at the stroke of a key?

Some images are too strong, and lines of decency should be drawn. But sanitizing war distorts the truth. Suppressing grim images because they might turn people against a war is deception. Governments attempt to do this as a matter of course. Reporters, photographers, editors, and executives should resist.

What finally ended support for the Vietnam War was reaction to a stream of flag-draped coffins coming home. Eventually, Americans had enough. Drawing the lesson, the Pentagon fixed that. For 18 years, it banned cameras from the flight line at Dover Air Force Base. The reason given, that families objected, was plainly spurious. When the ban was lifted in 2009, families of more than half the victims wanted photos to document their loved ones' sacrifice.

Sometimes, photographers get an image through, defying censors. The next chapter looks more generally at censorship. When covering conflict, the mission is clear. One way or another, correspondents must reflect reality in all of its multilayered ugliness. Hi-Mom stories and sidelights have their purpose. Yet what matters most is the grit of combat, the pathos of innocent blood, and a hard look at the price of whatever that might be gained.

x

Even when war reporting is at its best, column inches and

airtime are limited. Correspondents' books, written with
hindsight and evocative detail, help readers make sense
of daily dispatches from fresh fronts.

Vietnam is an essential study for journalists and citizens
alike. Michael Herr's *Dispatches* is a haunting reflection
on the challenges and emotions of any war fought at close
hand. It portrays adventure junkies drawn to war and rear-
echelon types who rely on briefings. More, it probes the
psyche of reporters like himself who do the job right,
whatever their fears or demons.

Malcolm Browne's *Muddy Shoes & Red Socks* is neither
literary nor philosophical. It is a thoughtful reporter's
account of a multifaceted war that escapes usual frames
of reference. The book is rich in advice for reporters and
people back home. It shows that grumbling from executives at the top is nothing new. Browne details support
he received from Wes Gallagher, his boss at AP.

Despite pressure from conservative publishers and editors,
he wrote, "Gallagher's instinct was to trust his people in
the field implicitly until and unless the trust was betrayed."
Gallagher, a former war correspondent, knew he had to see
the war for himself. He went deep into villages to interview farmers and fighting men. Thus informed, he ignored
threats by the Pentagon, the State Department, and
President Johnson himself. "When reporters were wrong,
Gallagher himself rapped their knuckles," Browne wrote.
"But when it came to protecting their freedom to do
their jobs, Gallagher was a tower of strength. Would
that all American news executives shared that quality."

War in Iraq has produced a shelf of powerful works. Two
books by reporters then at the *Washington Post* play off
one another. In *Fiasco*, Thomas Ricks tells how U.S. troops
were encouraged as Iraqis shouted enthusiastic support
when they passed by. In *Night Draws Near*, Anthony Shadid
tells how he followed behind to interview people in Arabic.
Those same Iraqis roasted the invasion in ringing terms.
One told him, "I curse them for a thousand years."

Jon Lee Anderson's *The Fall of Baghdad* shows how war reporting is more about the fundamental aspects of disturbing the peace. He does "bang-bang" as well as anyone. Yet he layers in complexities that trigger it. With sensitive gauges, he probes the trauma that armed conflicts inevitably cause.

Anderson seeks out well-connected contacts and stays in touch over the years. One of these steered him to Dr. Ala Bashir, a plastic surgeon and artist. As a friend of Saddam, Bashir made sure Anderson's visas were extended while so many other reporters were refused entry or sent out after 10 days. He also spoke his mind.

Once he explained how deep fear had twisted the psyches of ordinary people in Saddam's Baghdad. "I knew that Bashir had taken a huge risk in saying these things to me, and I acknowledged this by thanking him and steering the conversation back to mundane matters," Anderson wrote. "Before we parted, he gave me a final piece of advice: "Listen closely to the people, and judge for yourself. But remember, the truth is to be found in what they don't say."

✕

Bosnia is a crucial study in covering conflict and what lies beneath it. Opposing forces stared each other down, with sniping and shelling to unnerve civilian populations. Roadblocks, sniper fire, and sometimes snow made going rough, but reporters could go anywhere they dared. Beyond armed conflict, Bosnia pushed every facet of humanity to extremes, from selfless love to the cruelest forms of indiscriminate hate. It made plain that the longer a war goes on, the less it is about the original causes that triggered it.

In the beginning, Serb zealots (not "Serbs," many of whom opposed the nationalists) were plainly at fault. They started it. Blaine Harden of the *Washington Post* snorted when people said the war was too complex to fathom. "Yeah," he once told me, "It's about as complex as armed robbery."

But Serb atrocities brought retaliation from Muslims. Before long, both had much to answer for. So did the Croats. As a result, nations that could stop it had an excuse to stay away: it was a civil war.

Martin Bell's book, *In Harm's Way*, says much about how Bosnia was covered. "Hotel journalism" is usually meant as a slur, but Bell defines it differently. He tells of life at the Holiday Inn in Sarajevo, reduced to a blackened hulk with no electricity and every door open to gunners in the hills above. Coming home at night meant skidding heavy armored Land Rovers around corners and barreling down the narrow ramp. In the flicker of lamps at night, with shared bottles of duty-free Cognac and conversations that range far beyond mayhem outside, reporters forged strong bonds.

Bell laments that he would rather have covered war the old way, taking time to observe and to produce work that need not be rushed to a satellite for instant transmission. The old way was slow, but it worked.

For many, the grandest war correspondent was William Howard Russell, whose hand-scrawled dispatches took weeks to reach the *Times* of London a century and a half ago. He wrote that famed line from the Crimea, which lives jingoistic cliché: "They dashed on towards that thin red line tipped with steel."

Russell's universal themes still resonate today. Alfred Lord Tennyson put his dispatches to poetry: "Their's not to reason why; Their's but to do or die." After World War I, Rudyard Kipling harked back to that: "If they ask us why we died, Tell them 'Because our fathers lied.'"

Lines such as those can tell us more clearly than disjointed "breaking news" flashes from Vietraqistan about how we might understand any far-off war. Most are similar in the end, with delusional people at the top and hapless victims at the bottom. A reporter needs to cover both.

Censors,
Censures

PAGE 190

chapter thirteen

For decades, the University of Arizona's Journalism School has honored John Peter Zenger, the colonial New York editor whose 1735 trial established that truth is an absolute defense for libel. A British governor jailed him for eight months, but Alexander Hamilton swayed the jury. He was found not guilty after 10 minutes.

More recently, the school added tribute to Don Bolles of the *Arizona Republic* in Phoenix, who was blown up in his car in 1976. No one is sure why. His killer implicated a shady rancher and liquor wholesaler. But mob goons and race-track operators also hated his hard-nosed reporting.

Some days you can almost hear these men doing back flips in their respective graves. Zenger and Bolles may seem far afield from global reporting, but they are not. The common principles that drove each of them are too often lacerated by compromise, accommodation, and copout.

For as long as the world has had journalists, people have tried to muzzle them. We cannot begin to estimate how many, over the millennia, have been silenced by death, imprisonment, blood threats, or no more than fear of financial loss. Journalists worth the name resist. We talk broadly of the public's right to know, but the basic point is personal: reporters report, no matter what. In any given instance, however, it is not that simple.

No one can advise others on what risks they should take in doing their jobs. Courageous journalists have set the bar high across much of the world, where letters to the editor can come wrapped in explosives. But in the United States and Western Europe, where the dangers of defiance run more to irritated advertisers, nasty email campaigns, and cancelled invitations to the White House or the Élysée Palace, decisions should not be hard to make.

×

Russia is the extreme. The fusillade murder of Anna Politkovskaya in October 2006 focused attention on Moscow-style news management. Official links are hard to pin down yet hundreds of journalists have been killed mysteriously since the early 1990s. Death tolls are a measurable extreme. But there are countless others like Mikhail Beketov, beaten so badly in 2008 that he cannot speak a clear sentence.

His fingers were bashed – three had to be amputated – and he is now in a wheelchair. Police promised to investigate but did essentially nothing.

In Mexico, dozens have been shot to death, often in broad daylight. When threats failed to silence others, drug lords found a more effective tactic. They offered a choice. Journalists could accept a substantial cash gift to write favorable articles – or their families would be killed. In Honduras, seven journalists were methodically murdered over a two-month period early in 2010.

Elsewhere, the list is long. The Committee to Protect Journalists (www.cpj.org) publishes an annual report, *Attacks on the Press*. It is never pleasant reading, but in 2009 it was sickening. In the Philippines alone, 31 journalists were executed as they covered a political march in the island of Mindanao. Nine of Somalia's few journalists were killed and dozens more have fled the country. Worldwide, the death toll was 70, three more than in 2008, and CPJ was investigating 24 other cases. Iran alone imprisons an average of 65 journalists a year.

The days of "name and shame" are ending with the Internet age, CPJ executive director Joel Simon wrote in the introduction. In past decades, an editorial in *The New York Times* or *Washington Post* was enough to mobilize public opinion against repressive governments. Now bringing pressure is far more complex.

Little-known freelancers or travelers who post their work as "citizen foreign correspondents" are often suspect to paranoid regimes. They risk imprisonment or worse without major organizations behind them. The danger increases from rebel groups or bandit gangs who care little about what distant foreigners think.

×

Censorship comes in too many forms to fit into clear categories. Physical assault, happily, is the least common.

Far more common is what we saw in the previous chapter: government officials and military commanders keep reporters away from the story. This is most obvious in wartime. But it is part of a far larger problem, so pervasive that few of us recognize it even when it is happening to us.

Soldiers, as a rule, don't like to be second-guessed. They hate sharing battlefields with loose-cannon civilians carrying cameras and notebooks. But mostly, generals want to control the overall message and the sidelights that shape public attitudes. Their budgets and political clout at home depend on it.

After the first Gulf War, Hedrick Smith edited a book of essays, *The Media and the Gulf War*. His preface went beyond battlefields. He recalled how in the 1970s mysterious glitches disrupted communications whenever his Moscow reporting for *The New York Times* displeased the Kremlin. But that was not the worst of it. Smith wrote:

"... The most effective censorship of all is not the deleting of words, sentences, and paragraphs but the denial of access – stopping information at the source before I could learn it, simply putting 40 percent of the country off-limits to Americans and other Western reporters, and in all the other 60 percent, simply shutting reporters off from contact with Soviet officials and intimidating ordinary citizens so they would not dare talk with foreign reporters. I learned that the Iron Curtain was at my fingertips."

He makes a good point. Until the early 1970s, Western reporters could not get to Beijing, let alone anywhere else in the country. Today, Tibet and other sensitive areas are still hard to penetrate. North Korea and Myanmar are open only to rare controlled tourism. Iran slams shut its borders when things get restive. Russia, which for a while opened widely after the Iron Curtain fell, can be maddeningly opaque. Visas to scores of other countries run from difficult to impossible.

China is brazen about its censorship, not only keeping

reporters from sensitive areas but also erecting road-blocks in cyberspace. Website addresses often come up blank. Word searches for innocuous little nouns are blocked when they share a Chinese character with someone or something on the blacklist. Journalists find themselves hacked to bits.

University of Toronto specialists found interference targeted at, among others, Tibetan rights advocates and foreign journalists who write about Taiwan. In the old days, it was easier for reporters to spot goons in badly cut jackets who followed them on assignments or those clicking noises on telephone lines.

China's impenetrable visa policy is some carrot and a lot of stick, as the *Washington Post* learned the hard way. The *Post* needed a Beijing correspondent in 2009 and hired Andrew Higgins from *The Wall Street Journal*. But editors did not first feel out Chinese authorities. Higgins had done too good a job covering Tiananmen Square in the 1980s. He was later expelled. Party leaders were not eager to see him back. A *Post* reporter with high-level contacts found a way to get Higgins a visa. Meantime, however, the paper applied formally to the Washington embassy, which blocked backdoor channels. *Post* editors called on such intermediaries as Henry Kissinger without success.

Yet for all of this, there is a more insidious censorship: that which news organizations and individual journalists impose on themselves. Such things are hard to measure, but one of the countries where self-censorship is the most pervasive — when it comes to foreign affairs — is the one that sees itself as a global champion of press freedom: the United States.

Obviously, plenty of Washington-based reporters dig hard. Dana Priest of the *Washington Post*, for instance, won a Pulitzer in 2006 by working sources at home and following them abroad. She revealed how the CIA handed over prisoners to countries with no compunctions against tor-ture. And much of the problem stems more from self-delusion than self-censorship. Yet the pressure is enormous to go along, to avoid upsetting the handful of people who decide who gets prized access and who does not.

News executives in a highly competitive market want the appearance of an inside track. Beat reporters who are shut out of the loop fall by the wayside. With television cameras relaying news conferences to a Greek chorus of 307 million citizens, what we used to call "the working press" is now also a performance troupe. And adminis-tration officials run the show.

Take the case of Helen Thomas, who covered U.S. presi-dents for UPI since John F. Kennedy in 1961. Thomas knew what lay beneath every rock in Washington and how America fit into a wider world. In 2000, she quit down-the-middle agency work to write a column for Hearst. As Bush steam-rolled toward war, she demanded clear answers to the obvious questions. For newcomers to the performance, however, she was a batty old eccentric, humored by young colleagues and a condescending president.

In 2010, at 89, she was still at it in a changed world of ubiquitous amateur cameras that made American journalism a spectator sport. A White House visitor stuck a micro-phone at her and asked an impossibly vague question: What did she think of Israel? She said Israelis should get out of Palestine. Then she said they should go back to Europe or America. Did she mean West Bank settlers or legitimate Israelis? The citizen journalist did not ask.

Thomas' off-the-cuff remark went viral, accompanied by a horribly unflattering portrait. People who had never read a word of her copy linked her to Halloween. After a lifetime of admirable work, she retired in disgrace. Maybe it was time. But a Salem witch trial by a howling mob of censors and censurers should not be the determining factor.

Helen Thomas is an extreme case. Yet the two Knight Ridder reporters who warned of overlooked dangers in Iraq were equally ignored. The chain had no newspaper in

Washington, and their reporting remained faint discord in the background.

The deeply rooted dichotomy between the Washington press corps and foreign correspondents is not likely to change soon. But anyone who covers or consumes global news must understand it. Each is fundamental to the big picture. Washington reporters must reflect what an administration and Congress perceive, the presumed state of affairs on which policy is made. Correspondents must add a hard look at ground truth so policy might be based on reality.

×

It is bad enough when reporters or editors pull punches for better access and tell themselves a potential scoop is worth the compromise. Too often, the reason is simply some executive's fear that reader and advertiser reaction might dent the profits.

Among the most troubling aspects of Bill Moyers' documentary, *Buying the War*, were those memos from publishers who told editors to back off from questioning the Administration's zeal. This is a dramatic example of what we now see all too frequently, fear in the face of undefined repercussion. Seen in the light of sacrifices so many reporters and editors across the world make for the integrity of their profession, this is troubling. If spiritual heirs to the John Peter Zengers and Don Bolles bend under such little pressure, there is no need for censorship. Censure is enough.

Principles, in principle, are not for sale. But when the money is serious, executives often find ways to elasticize them.

Clark Hoyt, *The New York Times* public editor, examined the humiliating case of Singapore and the *Times*-owned *International Herald Tribune* when it resurfaced in 2010. Singapore sued the IHT in 1994 over an op-ed column that implied its leaders advanced by nepotism. The paper paid $678,000 and promised not to do it again. When an op-ed about Asian dynasties named former Prime Minister Lee Kuan Yew and his son, current Prime Minister Lee Hsien Loong, Singapore objected. The IHT paid $114,000 and apologized.

Hoyt noted the *Times* routinely applies the term, dynasty, to the Kennedys, the Bushes, and the Clintons. He wrote, "Some readers were astonished that a news organization with a long history of standing up for First Amendment values would appear to bow obsequiously to an authoritarian regime that makes no secret of its determination to cow critics, including Western news organizations, through aggressive legal actions."

A front-office statement to Hoyt boiled down to a simple point: Singapore is a big market. Ironically, the news came on the same day a *Times*' editorial praised Google for risking billions of dollars to stick to its principles in China. Hoyt concluded: "I think Google set an example for everyone who believes in the free flow of information."

×

Corporations and interest groups spend vast sums to influence news coverage. If these have no power to censor, many achieve the same purpose by manipulating facts to con reporters who are too busy, or not conscientious enough, to probe more deeply on their own. When all else fails, they can call in the lawyers to frighten a reporter's bosses.

Public relations people have always worked hard to sell their spin. One classic case was Hill & Knowlton's work for Kuwait. After Saddam invaded in 1990, the government in exile hired what amounted to professional liars to whip up support. Congressmen were suitably shocked when a weeping young woman testified that Iraqis had tossed babies out of incubators they looted from hospitals. Sympathy waned when she was revealed as a ringer, the daughter of Kuwait's ambassador to Washington.

Corporate executives spend heavily on press offices to handle reporters. Until recently, the style was for company spokespeople to answer questions, build relationships, and work hard to rebut any hint of bad news. The trend now is to stonewall, or, when cornered, to threaten legal action. Rather than taking the telephone calls to allow the essential human exchange that reporting demands, many provide only email addresses. Awkward queries can be ignored. Others can be brushed off with canned responses.

It is up to reporters to keep asking. With enough hard facts and critical quotes from people qualified to weigh in, a corporate "no comment" stonewall backfires. It has the air of a shady character taking the Fifth Amendment.

Stonewalling is effective when overworked reporters follow the path of least resistance. It takes time and effort to refute flimflam. And if a public relations campaign convinces enough people that brown is green, the few reporters who get to the truth can be smarmed as tendentious or at best eccentric.

That is what Hill & Knowlton did in Botswana during the 1980s back when few people outside of Africa had heard of the place. Botswana is a fine country, but democracy works there largely because 90 percent of the people are from the same tribe. It earns money from diamond mines, and much of its wealth goes into cattle ranching, a national pastime. But diamond mines and cattle ranches suck up scarce water. They drain wetlands in the stunning Okavango Delta. Boreholes deplete water tables under the Kalahari Desert, and cattle around them turn fragile land into dustbowls. This devastates not only wildlife but also the last settlements of San, the Bushmen. A few reporters wrote about this. But the government hired Hill & Knowlton to shape a different image, which it did well.

More recently, public relations campaigns allowed large companies elsewhere in the world to continue pumping greenhouse gases into the air and drilling for oil in fragile ecosystems. This is not censorship. But false pictures were created because news organizations did not do enough to expose reality.

×

In some cases, vetting news reports has a purpose. A military operation might be compromised, putting lives at risk. U.S. officers were correct in pushing Geraldo Rivera to what Fox News called voluntary exile for drawing a map in the sand of an assault they were planning. But censorship is wrong if its purpose is to prevent embarrassment. Reporters should be sure a censor's cut is not simply an excuse for officers to enlist them as cheerleaders. Watchdogs are supposed to bark.

Censorship, like other measures to mask reality, is meant mostly to shape a preferred version of reality. It is meant to intimidate, and it often works. Often, it does not. When writer Zeev Chafets ran Israel's press operations in the 1980s, he once cornered William Claiborne of the *Washington Post*. It would be a shame, he said, if the *Post* lost Israel's cooperation because of the tone of its coverage. It would be a shame, Claiborne replied, if Washington's main daily moved its bureau from Jerusalem to Nablus. The cloud passed. The subject was dropped.

During Zimbabwean elections in 2008, Barry Bearak of *The New York Times* flew into Harare on a tourist visa as many reporters did. Soon after, 21 police officers swooped into his room at a small hotel. When he was finally released weeks later, his long account filed from South Africa shed glaring light on exactly what Robert Mugabe wanted to hide about his dark reign.

He wrote: "I had never been arrested before and the prospect of prison in Zimbabwe, one of the poorest, most repressive places on earth, seemed especially forbidding: the squalor, the teeming cells, the possibility of beatings. But I told myself what I'd repeatedly taught my two children: Life is a collection of experiences. You savor the good, you learn from the bad."

Bearak was charged with "committing journalism," he said. "One of my captors, Detective Inspector Dani Rangwami, described the offense to me as something despicable, almost hissing the words: You've been gathering, processing and disseminating the news."

Happily, he was tried in a court that functioned as Zimbabwe once did. As evidence of the crime, the prosecutor produced an article scooped off his desk when he was arrested. It was by Anthony Lewis, written in 1989. The magistrate hid her giggle behind the sleeve of her black robe. Bearak was released, but his lawyer suspected correctly that he would be rearrested. A car sped him over back mountain roads to the Zambian border.

The ordeal in Iran was far uglier for Maziar Bahari of *Newsweek*. He was beaten and tormented so badly that he twice contemplated suicide. As he exited Evin Prison after 118 days, his captors warned they would track him down anywhere in the world if he talked about his imprisonment. But, once out of Iran, he let fly in elaborate detail. The headline, splashed across the weekly's cover, read: "What a *Newsweek* Journalist's Captivity in Iran Reveals About a Dark and Divided Regime."

Those responsible most likely paid for that excessive zealotry. It fit badly with the image Iran sought to promote: a just state being smeared by its enemies.

×

Some lines are difficult to draw. Ideally, reporters present observable bits of reality and set them among balancing quotes so that readers can make up their own minds. But this can be confusing. It is hard for people to draw useful conclusions about complex events in strange places halfway around the world. This is why reporting is a craft, if not a profession. A skilled correspondent lays in enough clues to guide the reader without tainting a dispatch with opinion.

News analyses, labeled as such, bridge the gap between stenography and editorializing. Reporters sift all the information at hand and then explain things according to their own fair interpretation. Done right, this is similar to the work of a judiciary. Personal beliefs and biases play no part.

For this to work, readers must learn over time to trust a particular news organization's logo. And editors who safeguard that confidence have to trust the reporters who are allowed to write news analyses.

After my AP reporting trip to Goma in 1994, I filed an analysis slugged "Bosnia in Black" that began:

GOMA – Listening to the tall, gentle school-teacher, I could have shut my eyes, mentally replaced all those syllable-choked surnames with others that end in "itch," and I'd be back in Bosnia.

The Rwanda killings were not the "tribal slaughter" of the soundbites but rather a spasm of something centuries old, ethnic enmity as complex as anything found in the Balkans.

One similarity stands out with blinding clar-ity: here was another orgy of genocide the world did not stop. In each case, at least 300,000 people died and 3 million others fled their homes in panic.

Both ethnic cleansings were systematic, pre-meditated by fanatics and spearheaded by well-organized bands of mass murderers.

But in Bosnia, there was lingering war. In Rwanda, it was a blitzkrieg of blood, scant weeks of savage hacking and stabbing by not only Hutu military people but also solid citi-zens run amok.

Soon after I sent this to New York, a note came back from the Foreign Desk. A top editor said some nice things about the piece, the note began, "but the moral outrage gets close to editorializing, he says, especially where we compare Bosnia and Rwanda as cases of genocide where the world stood by."

The editor had a point. There was indeed moral outrage. Genocide while the world stands by tends to produce that reaction. Was this too much for the AP wire? Genocide is a heavily loaded term, but it has a definition: a methodical attempt to exterminate people. I argued that in some cases plain reality ought to be presented as it is. But the story was reworked: desks usually win.

×

In a democracy, public officials are expected to protect citizens from distorted reality and safeguard the people's right to know. It does not usually work that way. Many classify crucial information not in the national interest but rather to prevent individuals from embarrassment. They punish zealous reporters by restricting access. Sometimes, they flatly lie. Such obstacles to newsgathering are bad enough when they hamper professionals. When authorities go after journalism students, they corrupt the principles on which democracies function.

In 2009, Cook County prosecutors turned the tables on student journalists from the Medill School at Northwestern University. For more than 10 years, the Medill Innocence Project has examined old crimes to find wrongful convictions. It has helped to spring 11 inmates. An Illinois governor said those cases convinced him to commute all death-row sentences.

But when students looked into the case of a man convicted in a murder 31 years ago, prosecutors subpoenaed the class syllabus along with students' grades, expenses reports, and email messages. A spokeswoman for the state's attorney's office told *The New York Times* that prosecutors wanted to know if students believed they would get better grades if witnesses they questioned gave evidence to exonerate the defendant.

John Lavine, the dean of Medill, called the suggestion "astonishing." He said he believed federal law prohibited him from supplying the grades but added that he would not do it anyway. Northwestern is fighting the subpoenas.

The case involves domestic reporting. But it reveals growing government pressures and what happens when the reporters and editors do not bark loudly as watchdogs are meant to do. It typifies a new trend across America. The Student Press Law Center's website, www.splc.org, lists hundreds of cases in which officials try to muzzle young journalists.

Students sometimes go too far. Libel is libel whoever commits it. But journalism schools need to train students to question authority, dig deep despite official displeasure, and push back against censorship or censure. Students who venture abroad face tough challenges at every turn. They cannot start out by being muzzled at home.

Staying Alive

chapter fourteen

When journalism is done right in much of the world, danger is part of the picture. The threat is sometimes over-stated, but there is no way to soft-pedal it. The closer you get to gunfire and explosives, overwrought mobs, fatal microbes, holy warriors of any faith, shoddily maintained aircraft in extreme weather, or crazed drivers on narrow roads, the danger grows. But until recent years, jour-nalists were seldom specifically targeted.

In an earlier time, authoritarian governments expelled reporters and sometimes jailed them, but few risked the outrage that would follow any suspicious death. Combatants of every sort saw correspondents as conduits to tell their side of the story. If you knew where frontlines were, you could keep your head down. Danger, to a large extent, was a question of bad luck.

It is different now. Bandits everywhere have figured out that reporters travel with lots of money. If held for ran-som, they can be worth a lot more. Zealots earn far more ink and airtime by executing a journalist than by both-ering with an interview. Governments simply dispatch hit men and deny any knowledge. Children manning roadblocks might squeeze a trigger without a moment's reflection. Terrorists once under some state control are now mostly formless and freelance.

Even in the Congo, during those early days of mayhem, I worried more about malarial mosquitoes and pathogens than drug-addled rebels with guns. I could try to guess where roadblocks might be and avoid them. If I traveled early in the day, before warm beer made soldiers mean and stupid, I figured I could talk my way through checkpoints.

But when rebel troops ran Mobutu Sese Seko out of town early in 2001, I realized the game had drastically changed. Rapid-fire assault rifles had replaced machetes. Soldiers who once glowered in frustration as we sped away now had four-wheel-drive power wagons of their own. And, more than that, levels of fear and loathing had risen exponentially.

As remnants of Mobutu's army fought Joseph Kabila's ragtag troops near Kinshasa airport, a group of us piled into three cars to find what was left of the frontline. After blast-ing at speed through the second roadblock, I reflected on our towering idiocy. Fleeing soldiers wanted three things:

vehicles, cash, and revenge on Europeans (read: whites) they blamed for their debacle. Here we were bringing them all three in a tidy package like a Domino's Pizza delivery.

We found the frontline and immediately wished we hadn't. I reversed my jeep and bounced off with a carload of soldiers in hot pursuit, firing at us. Ray Bonner of *The New York Times* sat next to me, advising somewhat needlessly that I step on it. Had they not gotten stuck in the sand when we left the road, someone else might be writing this book.

I have to admit, it was pretty exhilarating back at the Memling Hotel, as we all whooped it up over breakfast. But it was seriously dumb. And the craziest part is that I am not sure I wouldn't do it again.

Risk is part of the business. It is essential to understand and learn, as best you can, how to avoid it. Always keep in mind the basic rule: No story is worth your life.

×

Much good advice has been written about staying safe on the road, and it is vital to absorb it all. You'll find some websites and resources in the Appendix. For starters, page through a notebook-type guidebook produced by the Committee to Protect Journalists: *On Assignment: A Guide to Reporting in Dangerous Situations*. It offers practical counsel along with essays by old hands who have survived ugly encounters.

The Paris-based Reporters Without Borders publishes a regularly updated *Handbook for Journalists* with useful guidance, free online at www.rsf.org. The January 2010 edition counted 170 journalists in prisons for the crime of having inconvenient opinions. More than 800 have been killed in the past 15 years, and 90 percent of their killers have not been punished.

The group keeps a country-by-country watch on dangers facing reporters. It also offers manuals on first aid, insurance, psychological injury, protective gear, and training for high-risk assignments. If all else fails, it monitors a permanent SOS Hotline that accepts reversed charges: (33) 1 4777-7414.

Mostly, it all comes down to personal choices and common sense. When you go on the road, stay close to people who have been there until you develop a feel of your own. This sixth sense is indispensable, but it is also indefinable.

After Islamic zealots executed Daniel Pearl in Pakistan, a senior editor back home told me Pearl had been foolish. This man supervised the world's basic news report but had never worked abroad. He had no sense of what it was like to find truth in a place like Karachi. Yet he blamed Pearl for his own beheading.

It is never that simple. If you take every sensible precaution to its logical extreme, you might as well stay home. But if you don't do what you should to report safely, you are nuts. This is a life-and-death conundrum, and each of us has to define our own rules.

x

For all that is written about staying safe on the road, one thing overrides all. You must be able to hear the penny drop. For that, you need to be attuned to your basic instinct and have the confidence to listen to it. Initial guidance from old hands is fundamental. This is one of the many reasons why bringing home experienced journalists does so much damage to us all.

In 1991, when Iraqi troops crossed into the Saudi border town of Khafji, an eager young AP reporter wanted to get close. He spoke Arabic; it made sense. But I also sent along Greg English, an AP photographer whom I knew could hear that penny. Saudi troops waved them through the last roadblock. Suddenly, for no apparent reason, Greg slammed on the brakes, downshifted, and raced back down

the road. He realized why only when the shooting started. Greg had gone past an Iraqi outpost that he sensed
but did not see. He was gone before surprised gunners
could open fire.

So here are Rules One, Two, and Three. When your gut
tells you no, it is no. Forget peer pressure. Journalists
egg on each other, and themselves. That is natural human
behavior. No one wants to appear fearful. Company gives
the illusion of safety in numbers. Bullshit.

No one I have ever known could hear that penny like
Miguel Gil Moreno, a Catalan lawyer who decided he would
rather be a cameraman for AP Television News. He set
off on his own in Bosnia, in Kosovo, in Chechnya. His lens
took people to the depths of conflict, lingering on human
detail. Others captured bang-bang, combat footage,
but Miguel made it all real. He went places others would
not even consider going.

In Sierra Leone one morning four colleagues asked him
to join them on a trip up the road. They were seasoned
hands, friends from Sarajevo and elsewhere. Something
told him not to go. He phoned his editors in London. No
one insisted, but the message was plain: Well, if Reuters
is going ... He went, and we buried him near Barcelona.

×

Jon Lee Anderson, unsurprisingly, has wise counsel for
staying safe on the road. As a kid, he once flipped the bird
to some guys driving by in Brittany. They stopped and beat
him to within an inch of his life. After that, he learned to
keep himself out of trouble on the meanest of streets.
Anderson spends months at a time among the most volatile
and hostile people any of us can name. He can reel off
specific tips, but most of those are in the guidebooks.
Real safety depends on something more basic.

"The more you know, the more you have lived outside of
your culture and gotten to know other ones, the safer

you will be," he said. "Sixth sense, street smarts, call it what you want. An instinct for danger will serve you wherever are you. I know when I am in danger because a series of elements kick in. One of them is the way people look at me. I know if I'm suddenly with people who want to do me harm. If you're very inexperienced, you may not know that. I'm very, very cautious of people I meet for the first time in large groups on the street. I've been grabbed before."

Some guidelines help in conflict areas. For instance, never go down the road if you don't see peasant farmers or villagers around. "If no one is on the road, you're in trouble," Anderson said. "If you haven't seen anybody in a long time, you probably shouldn't be there, either. You might be in between front lines or in a mined area."

Americans, particularly, should be wary of exhibiting any sense of entitlement. "We're big, we're brash, and we tend to think our wealth protects us. These days, it does everything but that. It is very important to have all your senses open, to be circumspect, watchful, friendly. The main thing is to try to blend in."

War zones are dangerous for obvious reasons, and each has its own peculiarities. Quasi-peace can be just as dangerous. Daniel Pearl knew South Asia well, and he knew how to blend in. But he was after an important story, and someone he trusted offered to take him to see a crucial source. It turned out to be a trap.

In 2009, David Rohde of *The New York Times* faced the same dilemma in Afghanistan. The warlord he went to meet seized him as a hostage and held him for seven months in Afghanistan and then over the Pakistan border in North Waziristan. He eventually escaped over a wall to reach a nearby Pakistani Frontier Corps base.

The *Times* kept the story quiet until Rohde surfaced. Then he wrote a long firsthand account, along with multimedia presentation, which does much to explain survival techniques in such circumstances. Bill Keller, his executive editor, explained the paper's reasoning.

"From the early days of this ordeal," Keller said, "the prevailing view among David's family, experts in kidnapping cases, officials of several governments and others we consulted was that going public could increase the danger to David and the other hostages. The kidnappers initially said as much. We decided to respect that advice, as we have in other kidnapping cases, and a number of other news organizations that learned of David's plight have done the same. We are enormously grateful for their support."

By contrast, when Jill Carroll was kidnapped in Baghdad, also when meeting a source, the *Christian Science Monitor* mounted an ad campaign in the Arab world featuring Jill's twin sister. She was freed. Public pressure can sometimes work effectively; or it might only highlight a hostage's cash value.

This is not a judgment I would want to make. In the end, with Rohde and Carroll, all's well that ends well.

×

A crucial guideline in dangerous places like Iraq and Afghanistan is not to linger any longer than absolutely necessary. Traveling beyond safety zones is always risky. Even with smart planning, vehicles get caught in traffic or backed up at checkpoints. If ransom seekers or terrorists notice a likely foreigner inside, they can act fast. Obviously, danger increases when you get out to ask questions or to take pictures. Move on before someone with a cell phone can alert the bad guys. Don't line up interviews too early, and don't set a meeting place until just before the interview starts; it gives the bad guys less time to plan.

Opinion is divided over using armed escorts. Bosses tend to prefer them, despite the high cost. If calamity happens, they have done their best. Sometimes their insurers demand it. Indisputably, security cocoons have saved some lives. But they can be a severe hindrance. People you interview tend to be put off by hulking ex-commandos clutching semiautomatics. It is hard to blend in when you show up in an armored convoy.

Mainly, it depends on circumstances. When Somalia got ugly in the 1990s, we all used "technicals," young men armed with anything from hand-me-down hunting rifles to rocket-propelled grenade launchers. They added some security to long rides from Mogadishu to the hinterlands. But they could be more dangerous than bandits if they suddenly decided they needed a raise.

Once I caught a lift from Kabul to Islamabad on a UNICEF plane with other reporters. The BBC crew had a security man, a suave, sandy-haired ex-SAS commando. As we boarded the aircraft, Afghan soldiers insisted on looking inside his huge odd-shaped gear bag. They found seven antique rifles, all in working order, and they went nuclear. They accused him of running guns and smuggling artifacts and threw him off the plane. The U.N. liaison officer was livid; UNICEF was supposed to help children not traffic in arms. Luckily, Christiane Amanpour of CNN was with us. She upbraided the Afghans in booming Dari. We took off, but for all I know that security guard is still there.

Body armor poses a similar dilemma. When shrapnel and bullets pepper the air, you want to wear a vest along with a steel helmet that also protects your neck. When you are in a city at risk of the odd stray shell, such as Sarajevo under siege, the decision is less clear. It is off-putting to the point of insult to bundle up in Kevlar while interviewing people whose only protection is a cross or a Koran.

If you are too cautious, you may miss your story. Weigh each decision carefully. When in doubt, lean in the direction of safety. Reporting is not a test of courage. Many of us are chickens who nonetheless do what we must. Sometimes risks are unavoidable, part of the deal — but only sensible risks. Dead correspondent can't file copy.

×

At some point in the 1970s, it become fashionable to tape the words, "Press," or "Prensa," or "Sahafi," on vehicles headed into dicey areas. When helicopters and low-flying aircraft cruised overhead, those words went onto the roof. By the 1990s, most journalists settled for a single all-purpose label, easy for anyone to comprehend: "TV."

In some situations, that might stop troops or ragtag militias from opening fire. In others, I suspect, they simply give gunners something to aim at. Before you decide whether to mark up your vehicle, check carefully with colleagues who know the territory. Incognito may be the better option. More important, in any case, is to keep your vehicle on the road.

Road accidents, though not often talked about, are the greatest danger that reporters face abroad. Technology helps to some degree. Once correspondents spent hours on end with their hair standing up straight in mortal fear as a driver careened through crowded villages and over narrow mountain roads to get to a place where they could file their stories. Now satellite phones send words and pictures from anywhere. But harrowing rides are unavoidable, and traffic accidents kill as effectively as bullets and bombs.

Elizabeth Neuffer of the *Boston Globe* was as crafty as she was likeable, everyone's favorite road companion. When she began reporting abroad during the first Gulf War, I could see she had an inner guidance system, which she put to good use. She emerged unscathed from up-close reporting in Bosnia, Rwanda, and remnants of the Soviet Union.

In 2003, exhausted from back-to-back assignments in Iraq, she hurried down from Tikrit to Baghdad for yet another story. Her driver, hurtling down the road, made a wrong move at Samarra and smashed into a barrier. Neuffer and her translator died on the spot.

The list of such tragedies is long. Some could not have

been avoided, the fault of a vehicle that looms out of nowhere. "Road trip" can be a misnomer when there is no road, simply a muddy or snowy track down the side of a mountain. Speed is too often an inevitable requisite of the job.

Often reporters and photographers drive themselves, wisely or not. In some cases, there is no choice. In others, it is preference. But whoever handles the wheel, it is important to travel with a sidekick you can trust.

A smart priority on almost any assignment is to find a reliable, resourceful driver whose courage is tempered with good sense. Be sure you have some common language. Check him out for a few hours and then hire him for the duration. He (it is seldom a she) will be your best source, your confidant, your friend, your entrée to local culture, and, occasionally, your savior.

If he is good, he will steer you to facets of the story you would not find by yourself. If things get ugly, he is likely to pick up warning signals long before you do. Bargain hard. But whatever he charges, he is worth it.

Whomever you pick as a driver, check out the trunk before you head anywhere out of town. Be sure the spare is in good shape, and there is a jack. Look at the fan belts. Take enough drinking water, along with a jerrycan for the radiator and some cans of motor oil.

Politely slow him down if he scares the crap out of you but let him barrel if he has to. Some drivers take this stuff personally. At Cairo airport, I once climbed into a Mercedes taxi. The driver asked if I minded if he went fast. I didn't. He floored it and blasted through the first stoplight. "In Cairo," he said, turning around to grin broadly, "red lights are like apples. We eat them."

I was less indulgent with a flaming maniac who raced from Petra to Amman while furiously texting his faithless girlfriend on a minuscule cell phone.

AP's Wall of Honor includes Ali Ibrahim Mursal, against whom every driver anywhere ought to be measured. In Somalia during those grim days in 1992, I asked around about a car to hire. Ali showed up in a white Jeep Cherokee. Though unmarked, it seemed to exude "U.S. Embassy." Maybe not. This was Mogadishu, and I posed no questions. From the first handshake and steady gaze, I knew he was the man.

Soon after, we stopped at a sprawling open market outside of town. I walked some distance to talk to camel herders. Ali stayed with the Jeep, positioned for a quick exit. But a photographer traveling with us got nervous and ordered Ali to drive into the bazaar to find me. Quickly, a crowd gathered, and people began pounding on the doors. Ali floored it. With a slalom run among market stalls, donkey trains, and clumps of people, he got us out safely without leaving any victims behind.

Later, as I interviewed doctors at a hospital, rebels drove up with a wounded comrade. The photographer with me pointed a camera, and they told him to put it down. When he didn't, they backed us against a wall and stuck guns in our faces. Ali calmly talked them down, stroking the leader's beard in that curious Somali gesture of goodwill. Out of the corner of his mouth, he told us to get in the Jeep. We sped away before the leader's rage reignited.

One morning after I left, Ali accompanied an AP colleague into the market. Someone snatched his gold neck chain. As Ali reasoned with the thief, his partner shot him in the back. Ali got himself to the hospital, but it was too late.

×

Take no place for granted. For reporters who cover Asian mayhem, Bangkok is where they unwind by a pool. Gentle Thais in the "Land of Smiles" welcome visitors with colorful silks, flower petals, coconut curries, and corporal pleasures. Every so often, Bangkok is also deadly.

When South Vietnam fell in 1975, AP photographer Neal

Ulevich moved to Bangkok, where leaders feared a domino effect. One morning in 1976, he hurried to a riot by leftist students at Thammasat University. Troops moved in with withering fire. A UPI photographer barely survived a bullet in the neck. When Ulevich returned to the bureau, editors refused to believe his account. This was Thailand. Then he developed his photos of students, lynched from a tree and brutally beaten.

In 1985, Neil Davis, an Australian cameraman and a beloved legend, covered a minor coup attempt in Bangkok. For years in Indochina, Davis had waded into the worst of it, with his characteristic insouciant grin, and always emerged intact. In Bangkok, a tank inexplicably fired a round as resistance ebbed, and shrapnel ended his charmed life.

For weeks during 2010, the Red Shirts, mostly northern country folk who supported a deposed populist premier, paralyzed the heart of Bangkok. The Thai army responded with heavy weapons. Reuters cameraman Hiro Muramoto was killed, followed by Italian photojournalist Fabio Polenghi. Two others barely survived their wounds. Denis Gray of AP, who for decades covered combat from the Middle East to Southeast Asia, was certain for a moment that his luck had run out in his own tranquil home base.

The lesson is clear. Whenever and wherever there are men with guns, anything can happen.

×

Be keenly aware of dangers you can't see, such as microbes in food, cholera pathogens, anopheles mosquitoes, and other insects that can ruin your day. Water is now more easily purified, and chances have increased for an emergency helicopter ride to medical care. Still, careful precautions are essential.

In *Scoop*, William Boot's first stop before missing the boat to Ismaelia was a London outfitter where he acquired cleft sticks for dispatching his cables, a collapsible canoe, and a Christmas dinner for eight. At the old AP, correspondents went to stock up with Dr. Von Stein.

We called our friendly company physician the traffic cop. After an examination, he was likely to say, "You should see a doctor." No one left on a foreign assignment without his medical kit. It had enough Von Stein redbirds — Seconal — to help you sleep through cyclone season along with all-purpose antibiotics, power painkillers, and assorted diarrhea pills that could stop up Calcutta.

Being a hypochondriac packrat, I added my own stuff, from fungal creams to field dressings. And I still carry enough for colleagues who say they never get sick. Tough is tough, but a microscopic microbe can pole-ax the Terminator. If I didn't rely so heavily on carry-on baggage, I'd add more. It is smart, for example, to bring your own syringes in to HIV-plagued backwaters where they reuse needles.

If you take a particular medicine, bring more than you think you will need. Then put a spare supply in a separate bag for when the first one gets lost or stolen.

Stay current with your vaccinations and tuck that yellow health card into your passport. Some countries demand certain shots before they let through the airport. And you don't want hepatitis, let alone tetanus or typhus.

Once you assemble a medical and first aid kit, spend the time to learn what to do it. Hostile environment training courses teach the basics, perhaps enough to keep a friend, or yourself, alive until help arrives. That Scout merit-badge stuff is useful but only to a point. War-zone wounds go way beyond broken arms and blisters.

Plenty of guidebooks offer advice on eating in strange places. Not many get into what happens when your host in the Afghan hills produces that platter of off-color mystery meat atop rice and congealed lamb grease. For cultural reasons, smile and consume at least a bit. When out of sight, open the can of tuna you carry for such occasions. If all else fails, plead religious imperatives. Just try not to say you keep kosher.

Don't be too picky. Weird-looking does not necessarily equate to unsafe. Exotic eating is one of the real pleasures of reporting abroad. If something is boiled or cooked thoroughly over flames, it is likely okay. If it has spent a morning with flies in a market, reach for the tuna. Basically, be sensible and keep your Von Stein kit handy.

Soon enough, correspondents get to be diarrhea connoisseurs. Amoebic dysentery is not fun, a gift that keeps on giving as organisms take up residence for the long haul. But good old Montezuma's revenge is mostly a passing reaction until your body adapts to local flora. My rule of thumb is to be extremely careful if I am in a place for less than a week. Otherwise, I figure I might as well as be a temporary native. Talk to your doctor and decide.

Harrowing as all this might sound, it is meant to be precautionary. I know plenty of reporters who have worked a lifetime abroad with nothing more untoward than a bad oyster at La Coupole. Just keep in mind that old safe vs. sorry business and be ready for anything.

And this brings us to the larger question: What to take on the road? The short answer is: A lot. Just make sure it fits under an airplane seat.

Road Kit

chapter fifteen

Luc Delahaye, a French photographer of superior skill and mercurial manner, used to disappear into badlands for months with less baggage than most fans take to a ball game. That was when he carried film. Now a shoulder bag does it. He takes knockout pills instead of a sleeping bag. Once, about to fly off with a wounded colleague, he sent a friend to clean out his hotel room. The guy found only a dirty shirt and some toiletries, and he accused the hotelkeeper of theft. When he broke the bad news, Luc said, "But that was all I had."

Others exceed airline luggage allowances for a few days in Brussels. The range is broad between essential and useful. Creature comforts are important in lonely places when you can't get to the story. But mobility is paramount when you beg for a lift in a tiny aircraft.

A smart approach is simple enough: Pack money, maps, medicine, computer, phone, charging cords, and assorted bits. Take an absolute minimum of clothes with something, just in case, to get you into a presidential dinner. If you need to be reminded about the passport, be an options trader. After that, it all depends on where you are going and why.

If you expect people to be shooting at each other, for instance, this gets more complicated. Add body armor and a helmet. That medical kit needs heavy-duty bandages and antiseptic. Bring enough for your fixers and Luc Delahaye.

However you pack, some basic rules are important. Take all the batteries and meds you need. You will be surprised what you find in an African market, let alone a Berlin mall, but you won't want to waste time shopping. If you can travel with carry-on, do it. But if you must check a bag, add basic reference books and something for fun.

Traveling light lets you change your mind at last minute, grab the only cab when everyone else is stuck in baggage claim, and walk across borders without a gaggle of dubious porters.

For years, I carried my Miracle Bag, a carry-on fold-over in tough fabric that kept a suit unwrinkled with pockets for papers and zipped bags of stuff with which I could set up a three-man bureau. A chunky white knife with that distinctive cross, my Swiss Army refrigerator, could fix a Land Rover or perform minor brain surgery.

That was before 9/11. These days, if it has even a short blade, forget it. I've had inspectors take away cigar cutters that could not circumcise a cockroach. You will miss that liter of 12-year-old single malt, even if you don't drink. It could persuade the goon at the roadblock not to ruin your week.

For these reasons, your kit is a tradeoff. The main rule is if you must move fast in dicey territory, shed everything you will not absolutely need. If digging in for a longish haul, make yourself comfortable. Take decent speakers for your iPod, foie gras for your friends, and whatever else it takes for a break from the story.

When Sarajevo was at its worst, I packed in kilos of linguine, garlic, and bouquets of basil. With a battered tin pot and a gas cooker, we made bathtub pasta for 25.

Technology has made things easier. Early satellite phones were the size of steamer trunks. Photographers packed portable labs, chemicals, and bricks of film. Television crews looked like Stanley's column penetrating Africa. Now miniaturized communications gear evolves so quickly it is pointless to describe it here. But still, packing right takes serious thought.

The mother of all packers, so to speak, is Gary Knight, a photographer who moves swiftly and effortlessly with enough kit to outfit a medieval Crusade. The standard advice, when in need of an off-size filter, a Cohiba Esplen-dido cigar, or a Toyota radiator, is, "Ask Gary." Just don't ask him for a tie.

At the start of the Gulf War, he and photographer Christopher Morris rolled into a forward U.S. Army outpost near Kuwait border in matching Cadillac Escalades to spontaneous applause from the troops. Later he switched to a monster Chevy Tahoe. His iPod, relayed by VHF to military radios, won friends who helped him all the way to Baghdad.

I asked Gary what he would advise first-time journalists off to, say, a month in India and Pakistan. He rattled off a list without pausing to reflect.

"Baby Wipes, unperfumed," he said. "When there is no water, you can't be without them. Cables and spares. You need a spare for everything. When you are somewhere hideous, you won't find what you need. Always Ziploc bags, for passport, cameras, film. If you get rained on, or wade across a river, or fall out of a boat, things in bags stay dry. Gaffer tape; you can fix anything with it. If you cut yourself, it's a bandage. To save space, I wrap six feet of it around Sharpies markers for two implements in one. Also, parachute cord. You can use it to hang up negatives, string up a mosquito net, lash a door shut, make shoelaces, tow a car — you can do anything with parachute cord."

He also carries knives and nail clippers but ends up replacing them after every airport security check.

Tiger Balm is always in Gary's bag. Photographers covering the tsunami put it on their upper lips to block out the smell of corpses. It helps for sprained ankles and knees, colds, sore muscles, and bug bites. "Just remember," he cautions, "to wash it off your hands before you go to the loo. Otherwise, you're in real trouble. Take it from one who knows."

He takes flip-flops. "Bathrooms aren't usually in your room, and you may be bathing where people piss," he said. "It can get pretty disgusting." And his trademark is a collection of kramars, Cambodian sarongs.

"You can always tell where someone started their career by the type of scarf they carry," Gary said. These might be Palestinian black and white, Balinese batik, Guatemalan huipils, or Tuareg turbans. They all work. "They are a towel, a jock strap, a hat, a scarf, or a shirt. You can soak them in water to keep the sun off your head, keep dust and rain off your cameras, or wrap them around your waist. But always cotton. That doesn't melt if it catches fire." Once after photographing houses that Serbs torched during ethnic cleansing, he found his kramar peppered with charred holes. Synthetic fiber would have ignited to flame.

Knight's camera straps are always leather, which does not get sweaty or hot and cut into his neck on long slogs. Also, those logos on standard-issue straps are not cool.

For clothing, he takes two pairs of sturdy canvas black trousers, five identical pairs of socks, five loose boxer shorts, and five shirts of the same color. He has about 60 shirts in all, made by his favorite tailor in India for $15 each. On assignment, he selects a muted color that fits the terrain, or white. "I don't like to lose time in the morning deciding what color shirt to put on."

Each shirt has two ample breast pockets, pleated to expand, with flaps that button securely. Knight's passport and wallet are always on the right; his light meter is on the left. He always takes one of 15 jackets, again identical, made over the years. They have two large breast pockets, two larger ones on the sides, and three huge pockets inside.

He always wears boots, never shoes or sneakers. The last thing you need on the road, he figures, is a sprained ankle. If traveling with military units, he takes brown boots; they wear black. In Muslim countries where one must continually remove shoes to enter mosques or homes, he takes Australian elasticized slip-off boots.

Knight restocks his medical kit in countries that don't ask for prescriptions: Cipro and other antibiotics for respiratory problems and gastric troubles, codeine or the most powerful painkillers he can find, sleeping pills, a malaria treatment, antiseptic, and field dressings. He always has eye drops and, for when diarrhea and plane flight converge, Lomotil.

And then, of course, there are a few books related to the story and iPod loaded with music that fits the terrain.

For camera gear, Gary carries Leica M6s or Canons, with 35mm and 50mm lens. He also takes a 90mm but can't remember when he last used it. He prefers a Billingham bag, which keeps out dust and rain better than others. Gary wears a waterproof watch but seldom takes binoculars, which can make you look suspicious. He listens to the radio on his Apple. In the Middle East, a small Thuraya satellite phone keeps him connected. Or he uses a broadband global area network (BGAN) satellite terminal.

When checking luggage, he likes sturdy cases that can take a padlock and a tough cable that attaches to something immovable. And like most of us, he is always on the prowl for the perfect bag. In Buenos Aires, I found a deep leather pouch with thong ties and a shoulder sling. The shop had only one. Gary made my life miserable until I gave it to him. A generous sort, he made up for it.

"For something like Iraq, I start looking like an expedition from the nineteenth century," he says. "I took two hundred liters of fuel, food and water for five weeks, four spare tires, air filters, tool kits, and a tent."

Gary is not much for body armor, but it can be indispensable. Even those crazy enough to depend on their luck sometimes must produce both to hitch a ride on military flights.

Before the invasion, a friendly U.S. officer gave Gary an infrared NATO beam to discourage pilots from blasting him away and a heat dispersal device to lessen the chance of attracting a missile. An Avis agent in Kuwait rented him that brand new Chevy Tahoe, white with six Bose speakers. "You know you're not supposed to take it into Iraq, Mr. Knight," the guy said, with a half smile. "If anything happens, bring it back." He did, barely.

After coating the Tahoe in vegetable oil, Gary threw dirt on it. He added U.S. markings and a regulation orange sheet over the top. "It still looked out of place," he said, "but it made guys think. Before they blew it up, they wanted to stop to see who was in it."

Gary's iPod sounds wafted across the open desert via a small transmitter. Six or seven Humvees full of music-starved soldiers followed close to him, radios tuned in. But the clincher was his Thuraya phone. "Some of these guys hadn't talked to their wives in six months and had had kids in that time," he said. "Between the tunes and the phone, we were in."

x

Not many journalists need to travel that way, but the underlying philosophy is important to know. Two simple rules apply: If you absolutely need something, you probably won't find it on the road. If you don't absolutely need something, leave it home. Beyond that, however, assembling your kit is a personal matter.

Think carefully about weather. Wide-brimmed hats are obvious for the desert as ponchos are for monsoon country. Pack cashmere sweater vests and breathable long underwear for sudden cold. Layers are easier to handle than heavy coats. You can adjust to temperature and, if necessary, leave something behind.

Always fit in with your surroundings, whether in the wilds of Helmand Province or on the Champs-Élysées. The less attention you draw to yourself, the better. And the more you look like someone who is aware of local tastes and sensibilities, the more likely sources are to talk to you.

Sometimes, it is a matter of expediency.

When the Soviet Union was falling apart, my Russian fixer and a local stringer took me on a midnight road trip from Tblisi in Georgia to Baku in Azerbaijan. I dressed neutrally enough, and at each of the countless roadblocks I feigned sleep to avoid questions in languages I did not speak.

That worked fine until an Azeri border guard poked around the trunk and found my high-tech knapsack. He hauled me out of the car. After an ugly night of questioning we were turned back to Tblisi.

And it usually helps if you don't draw too much attention to yourself.

During the Vietnam War, Hugh Mulligan found a gifted tailor, the Honorable Minh, and started a craze. Soon we all had our customized versions of the standard kit: shirts with multiple pockets that covered the front and ran down the sleeves. Rick Merron, a cool-hand AP photographer, designed a little pocket for Tabasco sauce. This extended to jackets, reinforced to carry flashlights, notebooks, lens, and filters, with clips for light meter cords.

Banana Republic, and then everyone else, developed these into the standard travelers' fashion items. They are pretty handy in some circumstances. In others, however, you do not want to look like a duck hunter.

Neutral clothes do not attract unwanted attention. Unless there is a specific purpose, it is best not to overdo local garb. You are not likely to fool anyone. But journalists do not exactly have a dress code. Look around the room at any press briefing, and you will see everything from three-piece suits to Bozo the Clown getups.

When the gang gathered at the Al-Rasheed Hotel before the 2003 invasion, Jim Nachtwey, the grand duke of global news photographers, wore what he always does: Levis and a white shirt. Ross Benson of London's tabloid *Daily Express* had on one of his costly tailored blazers and soft leather loafers. Peter Arnett, back in Baghdad, this time for an MSNBC video diary, sported a baseball cap.

What you don't wear also counts. In his book, *The Fall of Baghdad*, Jon Lee Anderson describes chaos at Abu Ghraib prison when Saddam Hussein freed the inmates to celebrate his 2002 election victory (100 percent of the vote).

Giovanna Botteri, a good-looking blond reporter for Italy's RAI 3 television came to him for help. She wore skintight white Armani jeans and a white shirt. Her cameraman was caught up in the mob, and men on all sides were pawing at her body parts. They gathered like wolves, laughing and pointing excitedly. An Iraqi agent told Botteri to leave — fast.

Anderson wrote:

"She hooked one hand into the belt at the back of my trousers, and we began to move through the mob, as the agent moved protectively ahead of us, pointing to openings and shouting at the men around us. Now and then some of the men moved in, and I could feel Giovanna flinch, or yell, as they grabbed her. At one point she quipped, 'I don't think it was a good day to wear Armani.'"

Not really. The story gets worse until both finally reached safety.

×

In the end, you can always improvise or borrow kit. Travel documents can be replaced or, in extremis, finessed. The one essential is cash.

On big stories, TV networks bid up everything from rooms to fixers. Reliable drivers seldom cost less than $100 a day. They can run to $1,000. Authorities take advantage to gouge at every turn. Freelancers hoping to catch a ride are beginning to outnumber reporters on expense accounts. Even if someone is bankrolling you, credit cards, cash machines and banks are often useless during full-blown chaos.

Paul McGeough, a wily special correspondent for The Sydney Morning Herald, showed up for war in Iraq with $40,000 secreted away amid his various body parts. For large TV crews, that is chump change.

The biggest expense in the past — communications — is less of a problem. In the 1960s, a Reuters correspondent in Africa endured his bosses' wrath for not checking before filing at length by Morse Code. He paid a dollar a word at time when that was real money. Today, a dollar's worth of Skype time can fill a newspaper column. That is, of course, if you remembered to bring the right computer cables for your sat phone.

Visa?
We
Don't
Need
No
Stinkin'
Visa

chapter sixteen

Every profession has its version of Murphy's Law, which holds that if something can go wrong it will. For reporters, it is: The more urgently you need a visa, the harder it is to get one. A lot of countries don't require visas. You enter as a tourist and get a passport stamp at the border. In others, you declare yourself as a journalist and pay a few bucks. But then there are the rest.

As each country and case is different, few catchall guidelines apply. But the basic point is clear: get visas and keep them current. Without them, you won't get past airports or land border posts. At best, you'll simply be turned back. Sneaking into places like North Korea and Iran can get you a long prison term, or worse, for espionage.

Rules can change by the day, and some embassies have more leeway than others. I was once refused a Saudi visa in Washington and Paris, but the London embassy stamped my passport in less than an hour. I was transiting Bangkok when Rajiv Gandhi was stabbed. A visa would normally have taken a week. Thanks to a colleague, the Indian ambassador gave me an after-hours visa on my way to airport.

Here is yet another reason for keeping reporters based in foreign bureaus abroad. Correspondents need to make friends in embassies and consulates. Those who cover specific regions can keep current visas in their passports for some countries where news might suddenly break. For others, if they have mobile and home numbers for embassy people, they can call in a favor.

Before the first Gulf War in 1990, and again in 2003, a crowd of reporters gathered each morning at the Iraqi embassy in Amman hoping to waylay the visa officer. When he appeared, a scramble ensued for mass ingratiation. As human nature would have it, he responded to those he knew.

×

A lot of embassies refer journalists' visa applications to their information ministries back home. This means delay or denial. The usual dodge is to get a tourist visa, answering the inevitable question about profession with a vague synonym for journalist. I always like "contemporary historian." But this can be dangerous. As soon as you start asking questions, and your stories start bouncing back to the information ministry, you may end up in a cell somewhere.

At times, when the story is of overriding importance and time is short, you may choose to skip formalities. Do this only if you understand the possible consequence.

Every correspondent can bore you for hours with tales of crashed borders. My favorite is from the early days of Congolese chaos when a visaless Belgian correspondent strode across from Rwanda as police stood to attention. He simply pointed to the embossed gold "CD" insignia on his briefcase. It was the band from a Corps Diplomatique cigar he had smoked earlier that day.

In Johannesburg, some years back, an enterprising American TV correspondent made up a collection of visa stamps for African countries in case all else failed. It was risky to use them, but they usually worked.

When U.S. troops hurried to Haiti in yet another round of turmoil, I waited for two days at the Dominican Republic border. Colleagues whose editors had dealt with a Haitian expeditor drove in without a hitch. Finally, I sneaked onto a bus and curled up under the back seats as border guards examined passports. With the country in turmoil I could say I had come on a U.S. C-130 if asked later why I had no entry stamp.

If the story is urgent, the general rule is to move fast, get as close as you can, and trust your luck to find some legal way across the border. If not, make a judgment on what risks to take. Immediately after 9/11, Jon Lee Anderson scrambled to find an entry point into Afghanistan. He laid out his approach in an email to his editor at *the The New Yorker*:

As for visas from the Taliban to get into Afghanistan, this must be worked through their embassy in Islamabad. Peter says that journos, mostly TV crews, have already begun to swarm,

but the Talib are being noncommittal and taking applications and telling people to come
back in 15 days. He is working on a connection
inside the embassy whom he thinks is bribe-
able. (It might be possible to get a visa this
way.) If the shit really hits the fan, of
course, no visas would be needed. One can
always find a way to be smuggled in, as I did
before, during Najibullah's day.

To keep his options open, Anderson got a second U.S.
passport in London. The Talib would not be happy to see
a Northern Alliance visa, and vice versa. He, of course,
got there in the end. But he is not saying exactly how.

A second passport is a good idea as a matter of course;
U.S. and other embassies will usually accommodate journalists. But make sure border guards see only the one you
want them to stamp. Many Arab and Islamic states refuse
entry to anyone who has been to Israel. If asked, Israeli
officers will stamp your entry on a separate sheet of
paper. But ask before proffering your passport. Some
border guards take delight in slamming down that damning
stamp. A second passport also lets you travel while your
main one sits for weeks until some consul affixes a visa.

If you have time, work your contacts. Someone might be
able to help you short-circuit the channels. In such cases,
be careful not to tread on official toes. As the *Washington
Post* found out in seeking a visa for its new Beijing correspondent, who was blacklisted, backchannels seldom work
if you confuse things by also taking the more formal route.
Once a visa is formally denied, it is hard to get informally.

×

Visas are only part of it. Even in normal times, many authorities insist that journalists be accredited. In such instances,
it helps to have a letter festooned with stamps from an
editor somewhere. Even better is an official laminated
plastic press card from a brand-name government. The

French do a fine one with blue–white–red stripes under the photo, a number, and an ornate signature on the back.

During conflict and political upheaval, roadblocks tend to spring up like weeds. If guards can't read, even a New York library card might work. But do not count on it. More important is how you approach a checkpoint and how you answer often ludicrous questions. Be confident but not overbearing. Be respectful but not obsequious. On certain occasions it can help to be aggressive. But be very careful. If that backfires, you might pay for it.

Expect anything. When Nicolae Ceausescu fell in Romania, Blaine Harden of the *Washington Post* drove to Bucharest. Self-appointed guards barely out of their teens stopped him at a checkpoint. They would not have recognized a visa if they had been looking for one. When one found an apple rolling around the empty trunk of Harden's rented car, he placed it on the ground and stomped it into applesauce. Fortunately for all concerned, it was not a disguised grenade.

If you use subterfuge, be extremely cautious. In the first Gulf War, a number of us, allergic to pools, wanted to avoid military minders but still get to forward U.S. positions for the Iraq invasion. A photographer and I rented a Mitsubishi SUV and scrounged enough uniform bits to sail through Saudi roadblocks with a quick, sloppy salute. For U.S. checkpoints we wrapped cheesecloth around our heads. We avoided more rigorous controls by downshifting and cutting across the desert. But when stopped, as occasionally happened, we immediately produced press cards.

You might choose to obfuscate or to elude compromising situations. If authorities don't stop you, you need not answer their questions. You can be vague about the truth. However, one cardinal point is clear. For a visa, a checkpoint, or a control by police, it is not smart to lie about who you are.

New
Directions

chapter seventeen

Point your iPhone anywhere and touch the YouTube icon. Your potential citizen-journalist audience is in the billions, from Rockefeller Plaza to parts of Africa that Stanley traveled five years to reach. This is thrilling stuff. But imagine citizen surgeons at Seattle Grace Hospital. The metaphor is not so stretched. A scalpel slip kills one victim at a time. Flawed reporting can send rioters into the streets half a world away and speed hostile parties toward war.

For all the wondrous potential our new tools and tech-niques offer, reporting must be anchored on firm ground. Engrave these closing thoughts above your keyboard:

William Howard Russell's dispatches crackle with immediacy after a century and a half. Yet they took weeks to reach London. He brought down a British Cabinet and altered Europe's course. With instant communication, reporters could not head off calamitous war in Iraq. What matters is the message.

We have ditched the constraint A.J. Liebling bemoaned: "Freedom of the press is limited to those who own one." Anyone can file, uncensored, from anywhere. But it is now far easier to get things wrong. Reporters need training and editing. If pressed, those citizen surgeons could remove their own tonsils. But that is not a great idea.

×

Correspondents have always had to struggle to interest people in far-off news. The defunct *Brooklyn Eagle* used to have a sign on its newsroom wall: "A dogfight in Brooklyn is bigger than a revolution in China." These days, it is harder than ever.

AP polls editors each year to rank 20 top stories. In 2009, the first five were domestic. Afghanistan came in sixth, just above Michael Jackson's death. Iraq was 16th. A separate AP poll tabulated votes via Facebook. Iran, the only non-U.S. story, was ninth. Jackson was third.

Pew researchers tallied play in 52 news organizations, print and broadcast, during 2009. Michael Jackson beat out Pakistan, 1.4 percent to 1.2 percent. Global warming totaled .4 percent of the news hole. China was only .7 percent.

People who want reliable global reporting must look for it.
But where? In assessing the options, we tend to judge
by generality. So much is wrong with some once-trusted
name brands that many critics tar them all. But rather
than dismiss an entire "mainstream," we are better off
helping to strengthen newspapers and broadcasters that
still take world news seriously.

Danny Schechter champions the alternatives. Rumpled with
a scraggly beard, always laughing and often in a T-shirt
reading, "Danny Schechter, the News Dissector," he punc-
tures pomposity wherever he finds it. He is one of those
grand characters that America produces, an I.F. Stone
of the cyber age. He was an Emmy-winning producer at
ABC News' 20/20, a Nieman fellow at Harvard, and he helped
start CNN. His Mediachannel.org, scrutinizes coverage with
useful snacks for thought.

We agree on a lot but not on traditional news media. I
worry about scope. Space is unlimited for independent
newcomers. Yet, however good, they offer the bits of a
mosaic that they can cover by themselves. This leaves
out an overall frame.

Schechter's book, *When News Lies: Media Complicity and
the Iraq War*, has a preface signed, "Dahr Jamail, Iraq War
Correspondent." He writes:

"My coverage of Iraq differs greatly from that provided
by corporate media because I work to show how the occu-
pation has affected U.S. soldiers and the Iraqi people,
showing their dignity alongside their suffering ... The risk
is great, but worth it in order to work as a true journalist, rather than succumb to 'hotel journalism,' as Robert
Fisk accurately terms the method most corporate media
journalists now use in Iraq. While it is much easier to act
as a stenographer ..."

This troubles me. Hotels, useful when you need to sleep,
are magnets for local officials and shady characters with
much to say. You can leave them for the road whenever

you want. Some reporters in a larger team are assigned stay close to their hotels to attend briefings and keep track of policy blips that are part of the bigger picture.

Jamail is a fourth-generation Lebanese-American from Houston, a high-country guide in Alaska until 2003. He took himself to Iraq where he spent eight months off and on through 2005. His work, often informative and evocative, adds much to the mix. For depth, however, I'd go with a corporate journalist like Anthony Shadid, whose two Pulitzers attest to an uncommon grasp of the story.

Rod Nordland is "corporate media." He covered Iraq for *Newsweek* since the 1980s and followed the war until he joined *The New York Times* in Baghdad. Fearless, he wades into the thick of action. His sources run deep into Iraqi society and span a sweep of Arab diplomats. He is, in sum, an actual reporter.

×

We are beyond either/or. Jill Abramson, managing editor of *The New York Times*, defined where we now stand in an essay for the Spring 2010 issue of *Daedalus*:

"It is well past time to reject the artificial divide between the guardians of print journalism and the boosters of blogs, Internet news aggregators, and other new media. Rather than battling over whether bloggers are real journalists or whether newspapers need to be preserved, the fight should focus more on championing serious, quality journalism, no matter who produces it or where it is published."

Clearly, trends are shifting. Each year, the Pew Project for Excellence in Journalism compiles its comprehensive State of the News Media report. It focuses on America but also gives a sense of global directions. In 2009, it saw a shift away from "journalistic institutions" toward individuals. Spooked by shrinking audiences and revenues, news organizations join forces with former competitors. For global coverage, the danger is obvious. If one reporter gets it wrong, we all do.

The 2010 Pew report found most Americans did not value news enough to pay for it. In a society that spends billions a year on video games, many said they were too busy to keep up with the world. Yet another Pew report tracked Americans' evaluation of news media. In 2009, only 29 percent said news organizations generally get the facts straight compared to 55 percent in 1985. For the first time, more people said they get global and national news from the Internet than from newspapers.

Beyond America, trends vary widely. Worldwide figures show newspapers are gaining slightly in circulation. Many, however, are in deep trouble.

×

Today, we have potential we could not have imagined in wild dreams only a decade ago. Our challenge is to use it better. Substance ought to outweigh speed and fancy packaging. News as entertainment has always been part of the picture. Think of it as after-dinner crème brûlée, welcome on the table but not basic to sustenance.

Punditry serves a purpose, but it cannot replace the ground truth learned only by being there. We need skilled independent journalists. But we also need better big media. Approaches such as "crowdsourcing" add as much noise as knowledge. Remember that parable of sightless people describing an elephant by feel. They get parts of it right, but they miss the whole.

Training is vital. Out where news happens, inexperienced hordes create problems. Briefings reveal little when they are free-for-alls. Top-level spokespeople are few; when too many reporters compete for access, they favor the pliant and the easiest to fool. Military commanders clamp down when spectators overrun their battlefields. At times, you can hardly blame them. Reporters need to know how to fit in.

New ventures offer promise for a different sort of mainstream. ProPublica shared a Pulitzer Prize in 2010, the first ever for online media. GlobalPost gets steadily better. There are others. Some are likely to expand exponentially as they perfect business models and win trust. The best ones find journalists who cover real news in person and believe in getting the story straight. Others cut too many corners.

Not long ago, two young Arizona entrepreneurs sent me an email seeking advice. A fresh generation has no time to read news, they said. They planned a headline service. Since they could not afford AP, they would ask journalism students to provide "content." What did I think? I told them.

There are no shortcuts to real news. "Buyer beware" is particularly good advice when no buying is required.

×

As new media take shape, old ones must strengthen the foundations on which they were built. Nobody sensible can knock today's wondrous new tools. Writers used to pepper their copy with "TK" – to come – and then scramble to look up references and recheck facts. Answers now come as fast as you can type questions. Smart interns leapfrog from carrying coffee to designing new algorithms. (I just looked that up to be sure I knew what it meant.)

Yet these new tools drive us toward excess speed. True is a better adjective than fast. Today's you-heard-it-here-first mania is more about bragging rights than better journalism. When newspapers battled for circulation in the same city, agencies scrambled for even a minute's beat on big stories. The one that came first was likely to lead the paper. That counted at contract negotiation time. Now "breaking news" is a branders' cliché for wrinkles in a story that may soon prove erroneous.

Hits and feedback too often distort editorial judgments,

even at such solid agencies as Bloomberg.

As AP shifted direction, Bloomberg moved in from the edges. It was created in its billionaire founder's image, briskly efficient and businesslike. First it made money delivering financial data and economic news to companies that paid well. Then it hired a solid staff to cover the world.

At Bloomberg's posh New York headquarters, next to Bloomingdale's, row upon row of earnest people shape facts and figures into news stories. Each focuses on a computer screen rather than the world outside. It is the same in overseas bureaus. Bloomberg demands productivity.

By 2010, the new agency had defined its role. It wanted subscribers, and it tailored its report accordingly. Reporters were judged by the impact they generated. This is a problem for those who focus on those DBI (dull but important) stories that determine the world's course.

When the International Atomic Energy Agency voted in 2009 to censure Iran and demand that it stop nuclear enrichment, a Bloomberg correspondent filed a brief story. It got almost no hits, so he messaged he was going to lunch rather than file more. His boss sent a curt note to remind him that Bloomberg was a news agency. But insiders saw that as a sign of the times.

Columnist Caroline Baum wrote a tongue-in-cheek piece about efforts in Congress to create jobs, with a passing jab at Republicans' amorous dalliance. The hit-seeking headline: "Sex Addicts Give New Impetus to Job Creation."

This, one seasoned Bloomberg correspondent abroad remarked in private, is "crazy, self-contradictory and ultimately unsustainable."

×

All of the above will likely soon shape-shift. "Multimedia" is expanding like brooms in The Sorcerer's Apprentice. It offers fresh ways to take us across those cultural bridges to see and hear (and who knows, eventually smell?) distant reality. But it still depends on reporters being there.

Back in my journalism class at Tucson High School, Harriet Martin would have pressed her lips together and shaken her head at today's state of affairs. She taught us to raise respectable hell in our little weekly, the *Cactus Chronicle*, but only with professionalism. Looking back, I realize how much we absorbed pacing up and down as the printer up the street set our stories in hot type.

We learned to ask who, what, when, and where, but also why and what could be done. If we caught a stupid mistake too late, there was no going back. But those you could laugh off. I can still break into a sweat when I think about what might have happened had we transgressed any of those tenets and canons that Miss Martin had set in stone. Puny as I was, I think I could have taken her in a fair fight. But those pursed lips.

High school is where journalism education ought to start. Students need to know that facts are absolute and not determined by how many people agree with them; that opinion should be rooted in reality; that news judgment depends on a story's importance not its popularity; that nothing replaces being there. If something is wrong, you nail it whether or not your principal – or your president – likes it. You only have to be accurate and fair.

But many students learn the opposite. Not far from my old classroom, I talked about this with David Cuillier, a nationally respected University of Arizona professor who tracks such things.

"A lot of principals see it as their duty to teach students to do what the authorities say," he said. The kids of old rabble-rousers are growing up to follow paths of least resistance. "They don't even understand the idea of civil liberties and free expression in the press."

Finley Peter Dunne, a Chicago editor in the late 1800s, summed up this basic role: a journalist's job is to comfort the afflicted and afflict the comfortable.

As newspapers languish in the United States, they boom in other places. Technology brings global reporting to anyone anywhere with just a few keystrokes. When our familiar news sources let us down, we can look further. Newspapers from Barcelona to Beijing translate their websites to English.

If newspapers eventually fade away, it does not really matter. Times always change. Our grandkids will likely roar with laughter at the rudimentary tools we marvel at today. What counts is getting close to the story and reporting it in ways people far away can understand it.

For someone of the dinosaur persuasion, I am oddly optimistic. Plenty of young reporters are eager to pack their cotton underwear and go tell us what they see. The real question is whether they can survive out there. And that is up to the rest of us.

Readings
for
the
Road

chapter eighteen

Some of the classic books that are crucial reading for foreign correspondents require a reporter's skills to find. When I started out, everyone talked about *The Kansas City Milkman* by Reynolds Packard, a United Press icon who evoked that agency's famed dictum: Write so that a milkman in Kansas City can understand you. United Press has vanished, followed by milkmen, but that it still very good advice.

I spent decades looking for the book, later reprinted as Low-Down. Recently, the Internet miracle yielded two yellowed paperbacks. Beneath a ho-hum love story, it is a revealing period piece.

The hero works in Paris for an American agency (guess which). His obsessive bureau chief has fingers on every bulb in the City of Light. His reporters worked the phones but also ventured out the door. When an eager kid is hired, the wise old hero teaches him everything he knows and introduces him around town. The kid, a climber, glad-hands subscribers and sucks up to bosses. He is made regional manager whence he dumps on his mentor, who wants only to be a good reporter.

In searching for the book, I learned much from the flamboyant career of Reynolds Packard. Don't let anyone tell you the good old days were a perfect model.

Packard started with United Press in Argentina and covered both sides of the Spanish Civil War. He was in Ethiopia when Evelyn Waugh dreamed up *Scoop*. As war clouds loomed in Germany, he traded jibes with Joseph Goebbels at Nazi press conferences. In London during the Blitz, he declared unequivocally that Britain would prevail. His editor told him that was nuts but let him write; he was there. Covering civil war in China, Packard continued to predict outcomes.

Time magazine carried an amusing piece about a farewell party that colleagues threw for Packard in Peiping (Beijing) in 1947. "Their guest of honor had made their lives miserable with his peculiar scoops," it said. "The peculiarity of his scoops lay in the fact that so many of them were phony. His imminent departure made him very popular."

Packard told his host, a local editor: "I appreciated the story you had about me in the paper today. But I'd hoped that you would have the courage to say I was fired by the United Press. This is the fifth time, and it makes us even, since I've quit five times. And this is going to be the last."

It was. UP was not happy about a philosophy Packard once summed up: "If you've got a good story, the important thing is to get it out fast. You can worry about the details later. And if you have to send a correction that will probably make another good story." He told another group, "What I want to do is let my readers participate in my experiences in collecting news, whether it's real or phony." What a blogger he could have been.

Most likely, UP cut Packard loose because he cost them so much. That was why Walter Cronkite left to go into broadcasting. His biography, *A Reporter's Life*, depicts the polar opposite of Packard. After accurate, objective work during World War II and in Moscow, UP general manager Earl Johnson offered him the job of general European news manager. But Cronkite had a new baby. His $127.50 a week salary would remain the same, and UP was eliminating the London living allowance.

"In the face of my clear disappointment, he grew avuncular," Cronkite wrote. "'How long have you been with UP now — eleven years? Surely you must have learned by now how we operate. We take young men, train them, work them hard, don't pay them very much, and when they get good enough to get more money elsewhere, we let them go.'"

Soon afterward, Cronkite convinced KMBC in Kansas City to open a Washington bureau, and he delivered the news to milkmen via a microphone. Over the following years, eventually the anchor of CBS Evening News, he became the most trusted man in America. When he visited Vietnam in 1968 and came home against the war, President Johnson knew it was over.

When Cronkite died in 2009, a massive memorial service at Lincoln Center focused attention on the calamitous result of faceless corporations pushing aside responsible publishers. In his clear and simple voice, Cronkite's book explains what went wrong. Along with the "get mine" greed of the 1990s, news organizations suffered from confiscatory inheritance taxes and other levies that could be reduced across the board in the national interest.

And he concludes:

Newspapers and broadcasting, insofar as journalism goes, are public services essential to the successful working of our democracy. It is a travesty that they should be required to pay off like any other stock-market investment. To play the downsizing game, the boards and their executives deny to their news managers enough funding to pay for the minimum coverage necessary to serve their consumers well. They reduce the amount of expensive newsprint available until editors do not have enough space for the news they need to cover. Good reporters, writers, and editors are spread so thin that they cannot spend the necessary time developing the stories that the public needs and deserves. A more responsible press depends not upon individual journalists but upon more responsible owners. That is the real bottom line.

×

Whatever shape news media take, reporters still out there can master their essential skills, and citizens can learn how to evaluate reporting. For this, some crucial books can help. Few are specifically how-to manuals. But many contain useful clues and lessons learned the hard way.

A hefty book by John Maxwell Hamilton of Louisiana State University is vital background. *Journalism's Roving Eye* is, as its subtitle says, A History of American Foreign Reporting. Vastly researched, it begins with a 1729 mission statement from the Pennsylvania Gazette, "Account of the Method we design to proceed in." That was written by the

23-year-old publisher, Benjamin Franklin, who filled two-thirds of the news hole with diplomacy and foreign affairs.

"*The Gazette*'s attention to foreign news was not unusual," Hamilton writes. "Although the United States is today's dominant world power, with interests and responsibilities around the globe, the high-water point of foreign news — as measured by the amount of space given to it — was in the eighteenth century when America was a colonial appendage."

For a wider sweep, dip into a classic compendium: *The Faber Book of Reportage*, edited by John Carey. An anthology, it includes dispatches that were hot off the press, so to speak, in 400 B.C. Some of them seem as fresh as yesterday.

Thucydides covered the Athens plague in 430 B.C. and described overwhelmed rescue crews that had to dispose of bodies. "Resorting to other people's pyres, some, anticipating those who had raised them, would put on their own dead and kindle the fire; others would throw the body they were carrying upon one which was already burning and go away." Compare that to Haitians in 2010 who tossed bodies into old tombs broken open during the earthquake.

A few years later, Plato reported on Socrates' execution by hemlock. It is a richly detailed account, but the editor explains that Plato wasn't actually there. He had to find reliable sources who were.

The next excerpted correspondent is Caesar, with a one-sided version from 55 B.C. about how his navy captured Britain. Nine years later, Tacitus reported on Rome in flames. It is all there: atrocities as Spain conquered America; Boswell on Johnson; Darwin from the Galapagos; Victor Hugo on Louis Napoleon quelling riots in Paris; Russell on the Charge of the Light Bridge; Mark Twain on Americans abroad; Churchill on the Battle of Omdurman.

More modern dispatches start with Richard Harding Davis, who rivals Russell in correspondent lore. John Reed, Ernest Hemingway, and George Orwell weigh in, among a lot of others. Among the last is from James Cameron, the British master. As a freelancer working for *The Evening Standard* in London, he got permission in 1965 from Ho Chi Minh to visit North Vietnam. *The New York Times*, unable to get its own visa, carried his five-part series.

Other reporters covered bombing raids via official military briefings in Saigon and Washington. Cameron saw them from the business end. He describes a mock alert at a village bridge defended by pretty young militia women:

"It all seemed so palpably make-believe – this vital bridge defended by a chorus of sweet little girls; I felt awkward and rueful. And then, in the middle of the performance, the alarm went in truth, and the war game was real after all, in the sighing howl of jets overhead, the thud of ack-ack, and for all I know, for I could not be sure, a tiny volley from Miss Hang's young ladies in the foxholes …

"There were several such raids while I moved about the country, and it is fair to try to analyse one's reaction. It is not easy. What supervened, I think, was not the emotion of fear (for I was in no particular danger) nor high-minded horror – there was somehow a sense of outrage against civility: what an impertinence, one felt, what arrogance, what an offence against manners. These people in North Vietnam are agreeable, shy people, and very poor. Will this sort of thing blow Communism out of their heads?

×

Reporters' memoirs can be dull, but many are not. Browse and select what looks promising.

Whatever you choose to read, leave it at home. For the road, take a fat novel that has nothing to do with your story. When you file your story and no one is around to share the Jack Daniels, or your aircraft is delayed for the immediate future, you will want it. Trust me.

Mort's Rules

One morning before class, I batted out a simple list of things any reporter working beyond borders should keep in mind. Each is so ingrained in my psychic hardware that the project took only a few minutes. Over time, I reflected, revised, and bounced ideas off colleagues. The result is not much different from the original.

1. See it for yourself. This can be tricky with a moon landing or an undersea nuclear submarine collision, but you get the point. You've got to be there. If sealed borders or gunplay keep you from getting close, find the next best vantage point.

2. Find your fixer. Good local stringers with multiple skills are the backbone of global reporting. They help you get credentials, find sources, and score a solid vehicle with clean fuel. As translators, they are your ears. They take you into homes. On occasion, they save your life.

3. Think particular, not general. This is from Hugh Mulligan, a past AP correspondent for whom "legend" is no cliché. When I once wrote about refugees "with their belongings on their heads," he made it "with cooking pots, torn blankets, and bundles of sticks..." Better.

4. To be lucky, be where luck happens. You can trace this back to Voltaire: inspiration comes to the prepared mind. If you analyze how events are taking shape and expend the effort to follow your instincts, you'll find all the luck you can handle.

5. Check back, keep at it. Remember the Dag Hammarskjold crash. People make mistakes, and they lie. A quick check on the Web may result in repeating someone's mistake. Go back to original sources. Then double check with new ones.

6. Take names; write down numbers. You will be astonished at who suddenly gets to be pertinent to a story. Reporters are no better than their contacts. Nurture them over time. Remember if they like cigars or good chocolate.

7. Show interest. If you don't feel it, feign it. People notice when your mind wanders. If they think you don't care what they have to say, they'll stop saying it. And what emerges if they warm up is what you want most.

Some Further Resources

General

Losing the News: The Future of the News That Feeds Democracy, by Alex S. Jones
Journalism's Roving Eye: A History of American Foreign Reporting, by John Maxwell Hamilton
International News Reporting: Frontlines and Deadlines, by John Owen and Heather Purdey
The Elements of Journalism: What Newspeople Should Know and the Public Should Expect, by Bill Kovach and Tom Rosenstiel
Bad News: The Decline of Reporting, the Business of News, and the Danger to Us All, by Tom Fenton
Coups and Earthquakes, by Mort Rosenblum
Who Stole the News? by Mort Rosenblum
On the Front Lines of the Cold War, by Seymour Topping
Blood and Sand, by Frank Gardner
Citizens of London, by Lynne Olson
Foreign Correspondence, by Geraldine Brooks
People Like Us: Misrepresenting the Middle East, by Joris Luyendijk
Without Fear or Favor, by Harrison Salisbury
The Wayward Reporter, by A.J.Liebling
All Governments Lie, by I.F.Stone
AP: The Story of News, by Oliver Gramling
Kent Cooper and the Associated Press, by Kent Cooper
Breaking News: How The Associated Press Has Covered War, Peace, and Everything Else, forward by David Halberstam
Deadline Every Minute: The Story of United Press, Joe Alex Morris
Through Their Eyes: Foreign Correspondents in the United States, by Stephen Hess
Foreign Devil: Thirty Years of Reporting from the Far

East, by Richard Hughes
Of Spies and Spokesmen: My Life as a Cold War Correspondent, by Nicholas Daniloff
Witness: One of the Great Correspondents of the Twentieth Century Tells Her Story, by Ruth Gruber
News From No Man's Land: Reporting the World, by John Simpson
Buying the Night Flight: The Autobiography of a Woman Foreign Correspondent, by Georgie Anne Geyer
Flat Earth News: An Award-Winning Reporter Exposes Falsehood, Distortion and Propaganda in the Global Media, by Nick Davies
The News from Ireland: Foreign Correspondents and the Irish Revolution, by Maurice Walsh

Conflict Reporting

The Fall of Baghdad, by Jon Lee Anderson
The Lion's Grave, by Jon Lee Anderson
Night Draws Near: Iraq's People in the Shadow of America's War, by Anthony Shadid
Naked in Baghdad: The Iraq War and the Aftermath as Seen by NPR's Correspondent Anne Garrels
Standard Operating Procedure, by Philip Gourevitch
Embedded: The Media at War in Iraq, An Oral History, by Bill Katovsky
Fiasco: The American Military Adventure in Iraq, 2003 to 2005, by Thomas E. Ricks
Imperial Life in the Emerald City, by Ravi Chandrasekaran
The Forever War, by Dexter Filkins
Dirty Secrets, Dirty War: The Exile of Robert J. Cox, by David Cox
Muddy Boots and Red Socks: A Reporter's Life, by Malcolm W. Browne
Once Upon A Distant War: David Halberstam, Neil Sheehan, Peter Arnett – Young War Correspondents and Their Early Vietnam Battles, by William Prochnau
Reporting Vietnam: American Journalism 1959–1975, by

Milton J. Bates
Dispatches, by Michael Herr
War Torn: The Personal Experiences of Women Reporters in the Vietnam War, by Tad Bartimus, Denby Fawcett, Jurate Kazickas, and Edith Lederer
Chienne de Guerre: A Woman Reporter Behind the Lines of the War in Chechnya, by Anne Nivat
In Harm's Way: Reflections of a War Thug, by Martin Bell
The First Casualty: The War Correspondent as Hero and Myth-Maker from the Crimea to Iraq, by Phillip Knightley
Under Fire, by Jacqueline Sharkey
Hotel Warriors: Covering the Gulf War, by John J. Fialka
The Military and the Press: *An Uneasy Truce*, by Michael S. Sweeney
The Media and Peace: From Vietnam to the 'War on Terror', by Graham Spencer
Beyond the Front Lines: How the News Media Cover a World Shaped by War, by Philip Seib
Foreign News: Exploring the World of Foreign Correspondents, by Ulf Hannerz
Frontlines: Snapshots of History, by Nicholas Moore and Sidney Weiland
Unembedded: Two Decades of Maverick War Reporting, by Scott Taylor
War Reporting for Cowards, by Chris Ayres
Compassion Fatigue: How the Media Sell Disease, Famine, War, and Death, by Susan D. Moeller
Am I Dead Yet?: A Journalist's Perspective on Terrorism, by John Scully

Changing Media

The Al Jazeera Effect, by Philip Seib
When News Lies, by Danny Schechter
Digital War Reporting, by Donald Matheson and Stuart Allan
Free For All: The Internet's Transformation of Journalism, by Elliot King

New Media, Old News: Journalism and Democracy in the Digital Age, by Natalie Fenton
Newsonomics: Twelve New Trends That Will Shape the News You Get, by Ken Doctor
Alternative Journalism, by Chris Atton and James F. Hamilton
From Pigeons to News Portals: Foreign Reporting and the Challenge of New Technology, by David D. Perlmutter and John Maxwell Hamilton
Journalism 2.0: How to Survive and Thrive; a Digital Literacy Guide for the Information Age, by Mark Briggs
Managing Media Convergence: Pathways to Journalistic Cooperation, by Kenneth C. Killebrew
Information Age Journalism: Journalism in an International Context, by Vincent Campbell
Practising Global Journalism: Exploring Reporting Issues Worldwide, by John Herbert
Journalism and New Media, by John V. Pavlik
Journalism Next: A Practical Guide to Digital Reporting and Publishing, by Mark Briggs
Convergence Culture: Where Old and New Media Collide, by Henry Jenkins
The Changing Faces of Journalism: Tabloidization, Technology and Truthiness, by Barbie Zelizer

Photojournalism

Inferno, by James Nachtwey
Photographer, by Henri Cartier-Bresson
Requiem: By Photographers Who Died in Vietnam and Indochina, by Horst Faas
Slightly Out of Focus, by Robert Capa
Capa: A Biography, by Richard Whelan
Truth Needs No Ally: Inside Photojournalism, by Howard Chapnick
W. Eugene Smith: Photographs, 1934–1975, by W. Eugene Smith
Africa, by Sebastiao Salgado

Unembedded: Four Independent Photojournalists on the War in Iraq, by Thorne Anderson, Rita Leistner, Ghaith Abdul-Ahad, and Kael Alford
Farewell to Bosnia, Gilles Peress
Evidence, by Gary Knight
Photojournalism: An Essential Guide, by David Herrod
Photojournalism: The Professionals' Approach, by Kenneth Kobré
Witness in Our Time: Working Lives of Documentary Photographers, by Ken Light
Get the Picture: A Personal History of Photojournalism, by John G. Morris
Photojournalism and Today's News: Creating Visual Reality, by Loup Langton
Reza War+Peace: A Photographer's Journey, by Reza Deghati
War is Only Half the Story: The Aftermath Project. Volume 1, by Jim Goldberg and Wolf Böwig
This is War: Witness to Man's Destruction, by Moises Saman
Red-Color News Soldier, by Li Zhensheng
Digital Photojournalism, by Susan C. Zavoina and John H. Davidson
Visual Journalism: A Guide For New Media Professionals, by Christopher R. Harris and Paul Martin Lester
Photos That Changed the World: The 20th Century, by Peter Stepan

Film

"Buying the War," written and directed by Bill Moyers and Kathleen Hughes
"Outfoxed," by Robert Greenwald
"The Most Dangerous Man In America: Daniel Ellsberg and the Pentagon Papers," directed by Judith Ehrlich and Rick Goldsmith
"War Made Easy: How Presidents & Pundits Keep Spinning Us to Death," directed by Loretta Alper & Jeremy Earp

"Independent Intervention," directed by Tonje Hessen Schei
"Frontline – News War – The Complete Series", directed by Brent E. Huffman and Katerina Monemvassitis
"Citizen Kane," directed by Orson Welles
"Deadline - U.S.A," directed by Richard Brooks
"All the President's Men," directed by Alan J. Pakula
"The Year of Living Dangerously," directed by Peter Weir
"The Paper," directed by Ron Howard
"The Killing Fields," directed by Roland Joffé
"The Insider," directed by Michael Mann
"Live from Baghdad," directed by Mick Jackson

Practical Advice

Reporters Without Borders: www.rsf.org
Fact Sheet on Foreign Press Credentials, Society of Professional Journalists: http://www.spj.org/ijcredentials.asp
Afghanistan: *Crosslines Essential Field Guides to Humanitarian and Conflict Zones*, by Edward Girardet and Jonathan Walter
On Assignment: A Guide to Reporting in Dangerous Situations, Committee to Protect Journalists (www.cpj.org/reports/2003/02/journalist-safety-guide.php)
Society of Professional Journalists Ethics Codes (www.journaliststoolbox.org/archive/2010/04/ethics-links-1.html)
International Journalists' Network e-Learning (www.ijnet.org/ijnet/list/training_materials)
International News Safety Institute: www.newssafety.com/
Reporting Human Rights and Humanitarian Stories: A Journalist's Handbook, International Centre for Humanitarian Reporting
The Art of Access: Strategies for Acquiring Public Records, by Charles N. Davis and David Cuillier
Computer-Assisted Research: Information Strategies

and Tools for Journalists, by Nora Paul and Kathleen A. Hansen

Journalist's Resource: http://content.hks.harvard.edu/journalistsresource/

The Investigative Reporter's Handbook, 5th Edition, by Brant Houston and Investigative Reporters and Editors, Inc.

Career Opportunities in Journalism, by Jennifer Bobrow Burns

Flash Journalism: How to Create Multimedia News Packages, by Mindy McAdams

Multimedia Journalism: A Practical Guide, by Andy Bull

The World on a String: How to Become a Freelance Foreign Correspondent, by Alan Goodman and John D. Pollack

News University Free Course – International Reporting Basics (www.newsu.org/courses/international-reporting-basics-what-you-need-know-)

Organizations

Committee to Protect Journalists: www.cpj.org/

The Poynter Institute: www.poynter.org/

Pew Research Center for the People and the Press: www.people-press.org/

Dart Center for Journalism and Trauma: www.dartcenter.org/

Society for Collegiate Journalists: http://www.scj.us/

Newseum – Today's Front Pages: www.newseum.org/todaysfrontpages/default.asp

Society for Professional Journalists: www.spj.org

Center for Public Integrity: www.centerforpublicintegrity.org

Investigative Reporters and Editors: www.ire.org/

Student Press Law Center: www.splc.org/

International Center for Journalists: www.icfj.org/

International Reporting Project, Johns Hopkins: www.internationalreportingproject.org/

Project for Excellence in Journalism: http://www.journalism.org/
Overseas Press Club: www.opcofamerica.com
Frontline Club: www.frontlineclub.com/
Nieman Reports: www.nieman.harvard.edu/reports.aspx
The Freedom Forum: www.freedomforum.org/
International Journalists' Network: www.ijnet.org/
Journalist's Resource: http://content.hks.harvard.edu/journalistsresource/
National Freedom of Information Coalition: www.nfoic.org/
National Press Photographers Association: www.nppa.org/
Hearst Journalism Awards Program: www.hearstfdn.org/hearst_journalism/index.php
International Women's Media Foundation: www.iwmf.org/
Institute for War & Peace Reporting: www.iwpr.net/
International Federation of Journalists: www.ifj.org/
International Crisis Group: www.crisisgroup.org/
Feinstein International Center: https://wikis.uit.tufts.edu/confluence/display/FIC
Center for International Disaster Information – Situation Reports: www.cidi.org/sit_rep.htm
Panos Global Network: www.panos.org/network/index.asp
Essential Edge: www.essentialgeneva.com
News21, from the Carnegie–Knight Initiative on the Future of Journalism Education: http://www.news21.com/
News University, http://www.newsu.org
The Media Institute, http://www.mediainstitute.org
Reporters Committee for Freedom of the Press, http://www.rcfp.org
Association for Education in Journalism and Mass Communication, http://www.aejmc.org
The Media Channel, http://www.mediachannel.org